"Jennifer Eivaz has done a masterful job addressing .... the deep wounds and traumas we might experience. In this book you will find hope, healing and deliverance to live a life of purpose and divine design. Read this book and discover God's redeeming power for you!"

Sarah Bowling, founder, Saving Moses;
author, *Hey God, Can We Talk?*

"What you hold in your hand right now is an incredible gift. The weight of revelation in these pages is incredible. They are filled with such insight, revelation and wisdom for you to partner with the Holy Spirit through inner healing and deliverance to walk in greater manifestation of the freedom that is yours in Christ. Get ready to be untethered."

Lana Vawser, author, speaker, prophetic voice,
Lana Vawser Ministries

"Jennifer Eivaz, in her book *Inner Healing and Deliverance Handbook*, has created a very powerful weapon for freedom. Through her own vulnerability and darkest personal battles, she lays out a pathway of personal deliverance for every believer. Each chapter finishes with a prayer that leads you not only to wholeness and well-being, but to a confidence that Christ is indeed our great deliverer."

Pablo Botarri, author, *Free in Christ*

"Many people need not only physical healing but also emotional healing of the soul. This book places an emphasis on the hidden part of man that needs restoration. It will give you insight and revelation on how to minister to the inner man. Jennifer Eivaz has seen miracles in this area for many years and has done a phenomenal job in raising an army of believers to help those in need."

"Whenever we share testimonies of what Jesus has done for us, faith is prophetically released for God to do the same miracles for others (see Revelation 19:10). With transparency and powerful insights from Scripture, Jennifer Eivaz reveals how God has been faithful to heal the deepest wounds imaginable in her own life and in the lives of many others. These are stories of true, lasting healing and deliverance—and an invitation for every reader to experience supernatural freedom that is found in Jesus Christ."

"This is one of the most powerful, practical, well-balanced and healthy books we have read on the subject of inner healing and deliverance. Full of road-tested wisdom and truths, it is written in a very compelling and engaging way. Our friend Jennifer Eivaz has recounted with great vulnerability her own gripping journey to healing and deliverance and how the tools and truths she learned have then equipped her to very successfully be able to lead so many others around the world into their own healing, deliverance and freedom. This is an upgrade of wisdom that we all need in this hour, as a great harvest is coming in and with them an urgent need for freedom. It truly is our great honor to recommend *Inner Healing and Deliverance Handbook* to you."

"This is an awesome book! Jennifer Eivaz has given us a passport to begin the journey of healing and wholeness for our lives. The Lord has raised Jennifer up as an incredible example of a life delivered from demonic oppression and healed from deep brokenness. There has always been a tension between those who believe inner healing is the answer and those who believe deliverance is the answer. This book masterfully shows and guides us into the understanding that they both are necessary for our healing and freedom as believers. This generation is under an all-out assault from demonic powers, pain, fear and trauma. The Lord has raised up Jennifer Eivaz as an ambassador and voice of prophetic freedom. Her life is proof of what God can do! This book is a roadmap to let God bring the same healing and liberty Jennifer has into your life. It's so important that every believer is equipped to minister to a broken, bound and traumatized generation of hurting people. This book will give you the keys to unlock people from whatever prison they've been locked in."

Dr. Michael Maiden, lead pastor, Church for the Nations

INNER HEALING

AND

DELIVERANCE

HANDBOOK

INNER HEALING

AND

DELIVERANCE

HANDBOOK

Hope to Bring Your Heart Back to Life

JENNIFER EIVAZ

Chosen

a division of Baker Publishing Group
Minneapolis, Minnesota

Published by Chosen Books
11400 Hampshire Avenue South
Minneapolis, Minnesota 55438
www.chosenbooks.com

Chosen Books is a division of
Baker Publishing Group, Grand Rapids, Michigan

Printed in the United States of America

Library of Congress Cataloging-in-Publication Data
Names: Eivaz, Jennifer, author.
Title: Inner healing and deliverance handbook : hope to bring your heart back to life / Jennifer Eivaz.
Description: Minneapolis, Minnesota : Chosen Books, a division of Baker Publishing Group, [2022] | Includes bibliographical references.
Identifiers: LCCN 2021043499 | ISBN 9780800799229 (trade paperback) | ISBN 9780800762629 (casebook) | ISBN 9781493435791 (ebook)
Subjects: LCSH: Spiritual healing—Religious aspects—Christianity. | Spiritual warfare. | Healing—Religious aspects—Christianity.
Classification: LCC BT732.5 .E38 2022 | DDC 248.8/6—dc23
LC record available at https://lccn.loc.gov/2021043499

22 23 24 25 26 27 28   7 6 5 4 3 2 1

I dedicate this book to my King and Best Friend, Jesus Christ,
who paid the ultimate price for my freedom.
He was the supreme blood sacrifice, and one that turned
my world right side up and broke every chain.

I also dedicate this book to my amazing husband, Ron,
a deeply committed husband and father
as well as a faithful, steady rock in my life.
His unconditional love, support and encouragement have
continued to provide great strength for me.

Finally, I dedicate this book to my childhood friend Enrique,
long gone but not forgotten. (The details of his life and death
are described at the end of the book.)
His life and death settled my decision to pen a book I never
thought I would have the courage to write.

Contents

Foreword

As an ex–career criminal and convict who lived an extremely violent life, I know the absolute necessity of inner healing and deliverance. Even if someone hasn't been on the street or incarcerated in prison like I was, we all need inner healing. This world is unkind and brutal to all, no matter what color, gender or station in life. Any ministry that is not skilled in inner healing and deliverance will leave their flock dissolute, despondent and broken. My ministry is known for our fresh biblical revelations on soul healing and miracle working. In fact, many have called me the "apostle of soul healing." Although I would *never* claim that title for myself, it lets me know that healing the wounded soul is one of the most crucial revelations needed by the Body of Christ.

Being so immersed in soul healing has not only enabled me to see hundreds of thousands of people freed, but also given me the ability to recognize when someone else walks powerfully in inner healing and deliverance. Jennifer Eivaz is one of those rare people. I think there is nothing more destructive than when someone who dares to write a book hasn't yet lived out every line. This is definitely not the case with Jennifer. If you possess sufficient discernment, you will see that every pen stroke she writes here is a direct result of the scars on her soul and body. These are her badges that prove she has the legal right and authority to create a handbook on deliverance and healing. When you look at Jennifer with natural eyes, you would never guess that she has endured such high-level warfare. This proves even more that the extraordinary revelations contained in this handbook really work! Jennifer knows how to erase the scars, along with their side effects, and then remove the demonic landing strips they create.

Inner Healing and Deliverance Handbook takes you step by step through biblical precepts that will reveal to you the key issues in your soul and body that are causing the battles you haven't been able to overcome. In each page Jennifer gives you remedies that really work. When you're done, you will experience a supernatural shift in every part of your life.

Even after you work through *Inner Healing and Deliverance Handbook*, it won't collect dust on your shelf. This powerful handbook will always be your guide in every emergency and crisis you face.

Take a deep breath. Your freedom is here.

Big love,
Katie Souza,
founder, Katie Souza Ministries and Expected End Ministries;
author, *Healing the Wounded Soul* and *Soul Decrees*

Acknowledgments

I am so thrilled and honored to share my life and ministry with these great people whom I call friends. The thought of continuing relationship with those listed here for decades to come is comfort to my soul. This book was a hard book to write, the hardest. Their friendship and support are what strengthened me to write this book to completion.

Nathan and Elaina:
You are always steady, available, spiritual and faithful. I carry you both in my heart. I am so proud of you.

Joel and Mary:
I know when people have my back in every situation. Joel, you are always led by the Spirit and always steady. Mary, you are extremely kind and extremely fierce, depending on the need. Thank you. I cherish you both.

Catherine:
You are so funny and have a heart that never quits on people. I admire your tenacity to see hurting individuals

healed and set free, no matter how long that takes. Many people point to you as a key person that God used to bring them into real inner healing and deliverance. We are all much freer because of you.

Brad and Lisa:

I truly believe this book had much of its beginnings at your church, and I am so grateful. Thank you both for the hours upon hours of conversation. I look forward to many more Zoom times and in-person chats. Much love to you both.

Harvest Church Executive Team:

I have so much respect and love for you all. You are strong, wise, sensitive, prophetic, anointed, fun, very creative and the list goes on. You are the best team ever.

Harvest Church Eldership:

Thank you so much. Your support and counsel helped me to keep believing and trusting through my toughest season yet. You have also made leading a church enjoyable. Let's keep making history together.

Before You Read This Book

Some chapters and sections contain very sensitive content that could trigger traumatic memories, PTSD or dissociation in the reader. I have marked those sections in case you need to skip over the content or would prefer to read it at a later time.

To glean from the key points of those sections, proceed to the end of the chapter and read the prayer, the Kingdom Reflections and the Kingdom Questions. If you know you might be negatively triggered but still want the content, you might consider reading the more sensitive portions with your pastor, your small group or a trained Christian therapist.

Also, every story in this book is true. The names and identifiable details of the stories have been changed to preserve the privacy of those who shared with me the most intimate and difficult details of their lives.

Introduction

Several years ago, I watched a gripping spy thriller starring Gina Davis and titled *The Long Kiss Goodnight*. The plot is centered around a sassy and popular elementary school teacher in a small town, along with her eight-year-old daughter and boyfriend. The main character had been found washed ashore on a New Jersey beach, being two months pregnant and fully amnesiac. Having never remembered her real name, "Samantha" hired a number of ineffective private investigators over a period of eight years to try to discover her past. During the Christmas holidays, she is involved in a tragic car accident and hospitalized with a concussion. Then she begins to reconnect with her true self, a much more dangerous woman named Charly who informs her in a dream that she is coming back. Coming back meant Charly would be taking over her personality once again. As the movie unfolds, Charly is revealed to be a top assassin for the CIA, which is a far cry from her previously adopted small-town persona. The movie depicts her breaking free from her amnesia and returning to her true self. As expected, she goes after the bad guys with several violent and bloody fight scenes and plenty of explosives.

I watched this movie just once and felt strangely haunted by it, only I did not know why. I had thought to watch it again several times over a period of years but never did. With that, I would describe what finally became uncovered in my life as a feeling of being in some kind of movie. It was so unreal, yet it was truly happening to me. Through a series of events, I finally came face-to-face with my own severe amnesia. It was not quite like this movie, and in all humor, I am not a CIA assassin. I do know my name, I know where I grew up, and I can recall enough facts from my early years to put together a story of who I thought I really was. Still, there were large gaps of time in my growing-up years. I could not remember what took place no matter how hard I tried. I thought this was normal and never questioned why I could not call to mind certain years of my life.

Just like "Samantha" in the movie, at age forty-seven I had a missing piece of myself reemerge suddenly with an unbelievable story to tell. My traumatic amnesia had finally broken open to reveal its hidden contents. It was a horrific story that served to shake my identity so badly that I wanted to quit life completely. I had desperately hoped this was some kind of mental breakdown characterized by psychotic de-lusion. That would have been much easier to accept. This missing part of me, just like Charly in the movie, came out of my subconscious depths and gave voice to what happened during those missing years. Finally, I was facing the hellish memories I had made myself forget in order to survive the ridiculous.

Inner healing and deliverance ministry have always been an integral part of my personal growth as well as an effectual expression of Christ's ministry in and through my life. In reality, there has never been a time when I did not experience spiritual and emotional challenges for a variety of reasons. Every time something surfaced in my life that obviously needed inner healing or deliverance, I was diligent to pursue healing and work through my issues as best as I knew how. The problem is when your life keeps reflecting negative cycles and patterns (e.g., chronic sickness, mental breakdowns, frequent anxiety and nervousness, nightmares and night terrors, strange spiritual phenomenon, etc.), there is something within that is contributing to these cycles. There is some kind of hidden emotional and spiritual root system that will keep bearing fruit until it is unearthed and uprooted through the truth of God's Word and by the power of the Holy Spirit.

There are some who refuse to believe that Christians would ever need inner healing or deliverance ministry because this was all taken care of through the finished work of Jesus. They propose a philosophy like this: *We don't need to look at our past or what is wrong with us all the time. We don't need counselors or counseling. We only need to look to the cross.* Stepping into personal freedom, however, is not that simple for most Christians. Denial of your problems does not heal you, and what you do not deal with will eventually deal with you. Real freedom in Christ involves the process of facing reality and overcoming it with the truth of God's Word. I do agree that there are excesses among the ranks of inner healing and deliverance ministers that need to be addressed and avoided. For example, not every single problem is a demon needing to be cast out. I also believe it is the finished work of the cross that makes the process and journey of inner healing and deliverance ministry effective.

Jesus said, "And you shall know the truth, and the truth shall make you free" (John 8:32). Whenever we believe a lie, then we have aligned that part of our life with Satan, who is the father of lies. That part of our life cannot reflect the blessing of God until we make an exchange with God's truth, an exchange that always brings freedom. Too often, we do not know the lies that we believe. We might not even remember the circumstances that birthed those lies in the first place—that is, until the Holy Spirit reveals them.

My missing past began to unfold like an angry river of successive memories. I was so unraveled in response that I had to get help. This was not something I could walk through without the guidance and accountability of experienced ministers and professional counselors. The emotional and spiritual aftermath caused me to wrestle hard with the question, Can someone like me be healed? Just like the prophet Elijah, I have felt completely alone in my struggle. I simply did not know anyone else who had made it out this far, and I still do not. What happened to me is not something you want to talk about.

Ever.

And yet I am compelled to tell you my story and provide as many road-tested keys and truths as I can to help you heal, no matter what you are working through. This book that you are now reading is not as much of a method to heal as it is a journey with Jesus the Healer. That is how you walk out and heal from brokenness on this level, or any level for that matter. You have to equip yourself with His truth, and then let the Holy Spirit lead you into victory.

Pray this prayer with me:

Holy Spirit, I give you my yes. I want to be made whole, but I am scared and I feel weak. Help me to see past my issues and look to the many rewards ahead. Give me solid reasons to finish my healing journey and to never quit. Take the lead, Holy Spirit, and anoint me for inner healing and deliverance. Let every yoke be broken and enable me to help others break yokes, too. Amen.

1

Do You Want to Be Made Whole?

I was working part-time at a small but well-maintained nursing and rehabilitation home during my first year at Modesto Junior College in Modesto, California. It was an administrative position that paid minimum wage for minimal hours and without much responsibility. In other words, it was a gloriously low-stress job and perfectly suited for college life. My sole responsibilities were answering the phone and keeping an eye on things and only on the occasional weekend. Regardless, I was able to interact with some of their patients and was prompted by the Holy Spirit to reach out to one elderly woman in particular. I felt compelled to invite her to consider a relationship with Jesus.

I was a very new Christian, yet I could identify the voice of God speaking to my heart and mind quite often. His loving voice came to me concerning her as a clear prompting within my heart, but an urgent one. Immediately I began to pray in my prayer language and then drove the short fifteen minutes to the facility from my home. I found her easily enough, as she typically sat facing a window in her wheelchair, always bent over in an arch and never fully able to straighten herself up. I approached her as politely as I knew how and then shared with her about the love of Jesus and the power of His forgiveness. At the same time, I mistakenly believed she was ready to receive my words and did not anticipate what happened next. Instead of her being receptive, almost instantly an ugly stream of blasphemies and curses spilled out her mouth. She continued to make abominably vile and foul statements about Jesus until I gave up and walked out of the facility in both shock and embarrassment.

What was going on here? This usually quiet elderly woman was not crazy, as we are so apt to label people who behave how she behaved. She was demonized, meaning she was under the control and influence of a demonic spirit. We read about this phenomenon in the Bible many times, the most severe account being the man from the Gadarenes who was possessed with a "Legion" of demons, meaning thousands of spirits, all of which Jesus successfully cast out (see Mark 5:1–20). In much of American culture, which would also reflect much of Westernized Christian culture, we often misdiagnose or make excuses for people's outrageously bad behavior. We say things like, "She must be crazy" or "He's going senile," then fail to identify the real problem. This aged woman had a demon, and that demon hated Jesus viciously.

If I had understood better, I would have attempted to cast this foul demon out of her according to Jesus' own words:

"And these signs will follow those who believe: In My name they will cast out demons" (Mark 16:17). Demons are fallen angels who serve Satan, not God, and seek to afflict humanity in any way possible, which includes demonization.[1] Because I did not understand what I had encountered, I neglected to provide a true remedy. I also needed to know what Jesus had been anointed to do and why the Holy Spirit would come to rest upon us believers in the first place. It was certainly a learning experience, one I would never forget.

Jesus Is Our Example

In Acts 10:38 we see a beautiful description of Jesus' ministry while here on the earth: "God anointed Jesus of Nazareth with the Holy Spirit and with power, who went about doing good and healing all who were oppressed by the devil, for God was with Him." Did you notice how Jesus, God in the flesh, had to be anointed by the Holy Spirit to heal and deliver people from demonization? One would think He would not need extra power from the Holy Spirit just on the basis of who He is. Yet He kept pointing to a day when you and I would do the works that He did and even greater than He did. "Most assuredly, I say to you, he who believes in Me, the works that I do he will do also; and greater works than these he will do, because I go to My Father" (John 14:12). In other words, He had chosen to not be in a class all to Himself. We, too, can become anointed by the Holy Spirit just as He was.

In Bible times, people were physically anointed with oil to signify God's blessing or calling on that person's life. It was a physical act that coupled as a conduit of supernatural endowment or consecration all at the same time. People would be anointed for a special purpose (to be a king, prophet, priest, etc.), and the anointing would supernaturally change them into that role. When Aaron was officiated into priesthood, for example, he was physically anointed with oil in this manner. "And you shall take the anointing oil, pour it on his head, and anoint him" (Exodus 29:7). Likewise, the prophet Samuel poured a flask of oil over the head of Saul and anointed him as the king of Israel, an act that changed his heart into another man; he then anointed David king (see 1 Samuel 10:1–9; 16:1–13).

People were also anointed with oil to receive God's needed intervention in their physical health. We read, "Is anyone among you sick? Let him call for the elders of the church, and let them pray over him, anointing him with oil in the name of the Lord" (James 5:14). Even today, we can be physically anointed with oil for leadership in God's Church or for governmental roles. Just as Jesus experienced and foretold, we can become anointed by the Holy Spirit Himself for inner healing and deliverance ministry.

There is demonstratable power associated with the anointing of the Holy Spirit. The anointing is something tangible, not just metaphorical. The anointing will destroy what has bound you or confined you demonically. The prophet Isaiah described the anointing with this powerful statement: "The yoke will be destroyed because of the anointing oil" (Isaiah 10:27). A yoke in the Bible can be a metaphor to describe a heavy, burdensome task or obligation. In this passage, Isaiah was prophesying the future destruction of the Assyrians' heavy suppression against the Israelites and how the anointing would bring forth a national deliverance. King Rehoboam also used this term as he tried to terrorize his subjects into submission. He threatened them with "a heavy yoke."[2] Breaking a yoke in the Bible often symbolized freedom from oppressors. Demons may come to terrorize you and suppress you, but it is the anointing that destroys the yoke.

Anointed to Heal and Deliver

John the Baptist, a radical Nazarite,[3] had been waiting to see a prophecy fulfilled before his very eyes. John explained this about Jesus: "I did not know Him, but He who sent me to baptize with water said to me, 'Upon whom you see the Spirit descending, and remaining on Him, this is He who baptizes with the Holy Spirit'" (John 1:33). Finally, that day arrived. It was a day like no other. Jesus, God in the flesh, was baptized in water by John the Baptist. Then Jesus, standing side by side with John in the Jordan River, prayed a prayer that opened the heavens. The voice of God the Father sounded down to earth from the sky: "This is My beloved Son, in whom I am well pleased" (Matthew 3:17). Within moments, the Holy Spirit came to rest upon Jesus in bodily form and in the likeness of a dove. The Holy Spirit's arrival was a gentle one, but His fierce nature emerged almost instantly. He drove Jesus into the wilderness for forty arduous days and nights to be tempted by Satan.[4] Although weary and hungry, Jesus overcame every demonic temptation masterfully, being encouraged and strengthened by the angels who attended to Him. He then returned to His hometown of Nazareth, immersed in the power of the Holy Spirit.

As was His custom, Jesus went into the synagogue and read aloud to the attendees this prophecy from the book of

Isaiah: "The Spirit of the Lord GOD is upon Me, because the LORD has anointed Me to preach good tidings to the poor; He has sent Me to heal the brokenhearted, to proclaim liberty to the captives, and the opening of the prison to those who are bound" (61:1). He then proclaimed that this prophecy was now fulfilled in their presence. Pay attention to what He was anointed by the Holy Spirit to do—He was anointed to heal the brokenhearted and to set the captives free.

He also instructed those who believe in Him to go and do likewise, an instruction for then as well as for now (see Mark 6:7, 12–13; 16:17). This tells us that there is an anointing from the Holy Spirit to heal hearts, which is the foundation of inner healing ministry, and an anointing for deliverance from demons. This anointing will come upon people for personal heart healing and deliverance. It will also come upon people to minister these elements in power.

The anointing of the Holy Spirit is a destroyer of demonic bondage. Not only that, it pulls you back together in all of the places you have been broken. The emphasis is clear. There will be an anointing and a subsequent ministry in the earth that both heals broken hearts and delivers people. This anointing knows no limitations. It does not pick and choose what it will heal or whom it will deliver. Jesus came to give us full freedom and not leave us only half done (see John 8:36).

I have read and heard different testimonies from those who are anointed for this kind of ministry to others. Carlos Annacondia, for example, was a highly successful businessman who gave his life to Jesus at age thirty-five. Five days after receiving Christ into his heart, he experienced the Spirit of glory like a burning fire. Compelled by the Holy Spirit to preach the Gospel, he began ministering the message of salvation in small towns in Argentina. His ministry was marked by signs and wonders, the most notable being mass deliverance from demons. A mass deliverance is a type of group deliverance and "typically ministered to an entire group of people at one time. This is in contrast to individual deliverance ministry in which one person at a time is ministered to."[5]

Another is Ana Mendez Ferrell, author and minister, who died and went to hell, only to come back to life still not knowing Jesus. She was in and out of mental hospitals, tried the occult, lost her children due to instability, but then recovered when she encountered Jesus and became anointed for deliverance ministry. "Living through years of torment and depression filled me with a holy rage against Satan and his destructive work," she wrote in her book *Regions of Captivity*. "Setting souls free through the power of Jesus my Redeemer is one of the most important missions in my life."[6] Most inner healing and deliverance ministers became anointed for this work out of the issues they resolved in their own lives. This, too, is my story, many times over.

Stepping into Your Ministry

To clarify, every believer in Christ is in ministry. You, therefore, are a minister. A Christian is always an intercessor on some level, meaning you are called to pray on behalf of others in partnership with the Holy Spirit.[7] A believer is also a minister of the Kingdom wherever God has given you influence. This includes sharing the Gospel of Jesus Christ and operating in the signs of a believer, such as healing the sick and casting out demons.[8] We often categorize "real" ministers narrowly—as being those who receive a paid salary from a church or from a recognized parachurch ministry.[9] Real ministry is done by all those who have surrendered to Christ, paid or unpaid, recognized or unrecognized.

I bring up the necessity of wholeness in ministry, having learned that engaging any level of ministry or intercession draws attention to the condition of your heart. The prophet Jeremiah wrote, "The heart is deceitful above all things, and desperately wicked; who can know it?" (Jeremiah 17:9). I have learned the hard way that we really do not know what is in our heart, unless the Holy Spirit reveals it. At the same time, most of us are in some kind of spiritual violation of the Scriptures in some manner, either knowingly or more often out of ignorance. Unhealed issues of the heart and violations of spiritual laws are opportunities that Satan takes advantage of to hinder our lives and diminish our earthly ministries. He looks for legal grounds to attack and bind us because he is a thief and wants to seize everything we have. He also seeks to hinder any effective ministry from coming out of us.

With that said, I have had to be realistic and intentional to press into reputable inner healing and deliverance ministry as well as to engage in extensive Christian counseling and trauma therapy. If I am going to be an effectual minister and intercessor who lasts, I have to work on my heart. I had no idea that the countless hours of dealing with the messiest parts of my life would yield a book like this ultimately. As a matter of course, I have also become well-versed with the many streams and methodologies employed by inner healing and deliverance ministers, such as Restoring the Foundations,[10] Elijah House,[11] Heart Sync[12] and Bethel Sozo,[13] and I encourage you to do the same.

To get started, let's define the terms *inner healing* and *deliverance*:

> Inner healing is the healing of the inner [person]: the mind, the emotions, the painful memories, the dreams. It is the process through prayer whereby we are set free from resentment, rejection, self-pity, depression, guilt, fear, sorrow, hatred, inferiority, condemnation, or worthlessness, etc.[14]

It includes healing of the wounded spirit as well, something that occurs through parental rejection, occult ritual abuse and more. *Deliverance* is the process of casting out demons.

> Deliverance is from God and is part of the blessing of being in covenant with Him. It only destroys what is of the devil; it never destroys what is of the Holy Spirit. Since deliverance is a work of the Holy Spirit, it builds up the saints and edifies the Church. It tears down the strongholds of the enemy but builds up the work of God.[15]

My observation and personal experience with inner healing and deliverance ministry is that they work best together and not separately. To reiterate, the apostle Paul described Jesus as being anointed with power by the Holy Spirit to heal all who were oppressed by the devil.[16] There is a clear connection made in this verse between healing and deliverance. The elderly woman I mentioned earlier needed a demon cast out of her, but there was a reason that demon was there. There was something in her that needed to be repented of and healed, or deliverance from a demon would not happen or would not last. Always remember that sin opens the door. Demons gain entry points into your life either through sin committed by you or, in other cases, sins committed against you. The demon may have gained control of the elderly woman through doors of childhood or spousal abuse, occultism, drug addiction, rage, some kind of willful and habitual sin, or even something else. Unfortunately, people tend to focus on being delivered from demons without addressing why the demons had access to the person's life in the first place. Demonization may have occurred for one or more of a hundred different reasons, but these reasons will need to be uncovered by the Holy Spirit and then healed by the power of Jesus Christ.

A Greater Anointing Awaits You

Every anointing of the Spirit upon your life has a starting point and is followed by a season of learning how to walk it out effectively. That elderly woman in the facility was not the first person that I was sent to speak to by that familiar prompt of the Holy Spirit. Thankfully, I did not receive the same reaction from most persons that I reached out to in this manner. As these promptings continued, especially during those new years as a Christian, instinctively I spent a few moments in prayer, trying my best to hear the heart of the Holy Spirit for each person-to-person assignment. Over the course of years, however, I received similar internal pushes from the Holy Spirit not just to minister and pray for specific people, but to go on location and pray in various places. I noticed how everything I did had some kind of deliverance edge to it, be it ministry to individuals or strategic prayer for geographical locations.

I admit these kinds of prayer excursions can be harder to measure for impact. Still, when you know Him and you know His voice, you learn to step out in simple trust and pray the things He has brought to your heart to pray. This powerful act of partnership is based on Jesus' prayer instructions to His disciples and now to us, specifically to pray for God's Kingdom to come and His will to be done "on earth as it is in heaven" (Matthew 6:10). This kind of intercession creates a genuine heaven-to-earth connection and is intended to bring deliverance to geographical regions from territorial demons that have blinded its residents from receiving the Gospel of Jesus Christ. From numerous historical accounts, as well as from my own personal experience, it is clear that before there is ever a revival, meaning a mass geographical conversion to the Gospel of Jesus Christ, there is first an intercessor. That intercessor will understand deliverance not only on a personal level, but also for territories, and know how to bring deliverance on a regional level and beyond.[17]

At this point, you might be asking, *Isn't this book supposed to be about inner healing and deliverance, but more on a personal level?* It absolutely is! I brought up the lifestyle of an intercessor, meaning the traveling prayer assignments and intense intercession, to jumpstart a highly needed and more generalized discussion about wholeness in personal ministry.

Decide to Be Made Whole

Successful inner healing and deliverance is more about the journey and the process of becoming whole. It is not an instant fix to life's ailments because healing takes time. With that said, a person will need to have some airtight, rock-solid reasons to go ahead and heal. In John 5:1–9 we read,

> After this there was a feast of the Jews, and Jesus went up to Jerusalem. Now there is in Jerusalem by the Sheep Gate a pool, which is called in Hebrew, Bethesda, having five porches. In these lay a great multitude of sick people, blind, lame, paralyzed, waiting for the moving of the water. For an angel went down at a certain time into the pool and stirred up the water; then whoever stepped in first, after the stirring of the water, was made well of whatever disease he had. Now a certain man was there who had an infirmity thirty-eight years. When Jesus saw him lying there, and knew that he already had been in that condition a long time, He said to him, "Do you want to be made well?"
>
> The sick man answered Him, "Sir, I have no man to put me into the pool when the water is stirred up; but while I am coming, another steps down before me."
>
> Jesus said to him, "Rise, take up your bed and walk." And immediately the man was made well, took up his bed, and walked.

Jesus asked the infirmed man at the pool of Bethesda, "Do you want to be made well?" (verse 6). Why would Jesus ask a seemingly obvious question? Doesn't everyone want to be well? When you decide to go after your healing, there is always work involved. It takes work to confront and resolve the difficult parts of your past that you have never confronted before. It takes work to not only dig up deep-level pain and deep-seated fear but to hold steady on to God when your internal world turns upside down. Those unruly emotions that arrive with the process are not only temporary but exceedingly fierce. This is the reason you will need to remind yourself often why you want to be made well.

Right now, I want to provide you with inspiration to fully engage your personal inner healing and deliverance journey. God is eagerly waiting to design unprecedented beauty from your ashes.[18] When He delivers and restores you, He does so with an exclamation point. In addition, people you have not met yet are depending on your healing story. There is a far-reaching ripple effect that occurs when one person receives wholeness, healing and deliverance. It is a rippling that impacts not only the here and now but also entire lineages for generations to come. God spoke His promise to me, and I believe it is a promise for you as well. He said, *What beat others, won't beat you.* If your situation seems impossible, know that you are being kissed with a divine grace to overcome what others would not or could not overcome. You, too, are receiving the Holy Spirit's gift of faith, which is supernatural faith and not ordinary faith. With God's help, you will defeat the worst damage of your past, as long as you keep answering yes to His question, "Do you want to be made well?" (John 5:6).

MY **PRAYER** FOR YOU

In the name of Jesus, I invite the Holy Spirit to begin a miraculous healing work inside of your heart. I ask Him to provide you with supernatural courage and a divine ability to face what you have never been able to face before. May He give you the strength to overcome and heal from everything determined by man as impossible to heal from. I pray that you hear, know and believe the good word that He has spoken about you since eternity. May His love and glory utterly compel you to rise up from your ashes and dark places and soar to great heights in the Lord. In Jesus' name, Amen.

KINGDOM REFLECTIONS

1. Jesus, God in the flesh, had to be anointed by the Holy Spirit to heal and deliver people from demonization. Just as Jesus experienced and foretold, we can become anointed by the Holy Spirit Himself for inner healing and deliverance ministry.

2. It is the anointing that destroys the yoke, which is a biblical metaphor to describe a heavy, burdensome task or obligation. It will also destroy demonic bondages of any kind.

3. Unhealed issues of the heart and violations of spiritual laws (sin) are opportunities that Satan takes advantage of to hinder our lives and diminish our earthly ministries.

4. People might focus on being delivered from demons without addressing why the demons had access to the person's life in the first place. Deliverance and inner healing always go together.

5. When God delivers and restores you, He does so with an exclamation point. People you have not met yet are depending on your healing story.

KINGDOM QUESTIONS

1. How often do we misdiagnose demonization as mental illness? Can you cite any clear examples of misdiagnosis?
2. What is the purpose of the anointing? How has the anointing broken any yokes in your life?
3. Have you ever felt hindered in personal ministry because of emotional wounds and spiritual bondage? Why or why not?
4. Why would some people reject the process of receiving personal inner healing and deliverance?
5. Do you want to be made well?

2

Dead Hearts Really
Do Come Back to Life

(Content in this chapter is sensitive. Read with caution.)

I was ministering at a large and popular prophetic school alongside a small team of other prophets, a school that I had been involved with for a number of years. This time, I had arrived at the venue edgy and emotionally raw, having just miscarried a pregnancy the week prior. In my grief, I experienced a myriad of emotions—anger, sadness. Thankfully, the school and other ministers provided a healthy distraction, as well as some needed and private emotional support while I was there.

During an evening session, a guest prophet with a large international ministry was ministering. He was an outstanding and dynamic teacher and genuinely powerful by the Holy

Spirit. At the end of this session, the prophetic anointing seemed to pour like water over the entire room. The guest prophet began to prophesy words that seemed to flow like a fiery river. First, he prophesied to a young Ugandan woman who was desperate to know God's intended future for her life and her struggling nation. As he was ministering to her, all of a sudden and without warning, the anointing fell upon me like a giant splash of water, causing a sudden outburst of tears. He then turned his attention from the Ugandan woman toward me and began to prophesy into a powerful shift for my life.

He began shouting, "You have been intimidated your entire life!" This was all going on in front of seven hundred or more people, and I was immediately annoyed at his statement. For some reason, I felt exposed and vulnerable. He said a few more things along those lines before he said this: "I see crowds of Asian people. You will go and minister in East Asia." Next, he began naming as many East Asian nations as he could think of, such as China, Korea, Thailand, Malaysia, Vietnam, etc.

At that point, I was arguing with him, but only internally. *It's Central Asia, not East Asia. You've got the wrong Asia.* At the time, that was true. I had been ministering in partnership with an evangelistic organization to an underground structure in Central Asia. I had never desired to go to East Asia.

Then suddenly, the prophetic utterance took a deep twist and left me almost breathless. The minister said, "And your father . . ."

When he spoke that out, I went on some kind of subconscious autopilot. Not realizing what I was doing, I fully turned away from him with the intent of walking out of the building. I suddenly recognized I was in an auditorium in front of a large crowd of people and that my adverse reaction was all being filmed. With that, I turned back and faced the minister, but inside I was fuming. *Don't you dare bring up my father.*

He then finished off with a shocking statement. "And the ministry that was on your father is now coming onto you."

A Spiritual Inheritance Restored

I have only shared this occasionally in public settings, but I have never written this portion of my testimony down to be read by a wider audience. For me at least, once I have written something down for others to read, it seems to take on a deeper reality in my psyche. This topic has never been something I could wrap my mind around, either.

As I mentioned in the introduction, I have a lot of missing memories from my growing-up years. I can remember the highlights, such as my family of origin, growing up in the Mormon church, living and being educated in Modesto, California, the growing issues in my immediate family, and a few other things like that. At the same time, I have noticed these missing gaps of time, all leading up to one scene in my teen years that should have left me shattered. Instead, it became the catalyst for me to receive Jesus Christ as my Lord and Savior.

My biological father, now deceased, had lived and worked in Hollywood, California, since my elementary school education. I would visit him for a few weeks or more a year as agreed upon between him and my mother. He was an accountant by trade and worked in the financial industry of Hollywood. Besides joining him on a few business trips, all of which were a disaster in my opinion, my one and only memory of his work environment was a single visit to his office somewhere in downtown Hollywood. I was early elementary school age and recall riding up the elevator of the tallest building I had ever been in. I was quite awestruck with the experience, especially after seeing his spacious office, large desk and big leather chair.

At the same time, my biological father was an alcoholic, schizophrenic and quite unbearable emotionally. I was not sure how he held on to his employment with all that going on, viewing firsthand how out of control his drinking really was. I want to emphasize that there were these large gaps of time growing up when my memories seemed to have vanished, a phenomenon I will discuss later in the book. What I do remember is what happened during my annual visit to Hollywood the summer before my sixteenth birthday. It was the nightmare I could not wake up from. Literally.

I had fallen asleep for the night at my biological father's apartment. I cannot remember much more than this, but during the night, and like a horrible nightmare, I was forcibly subjected to an aggressive rape. I could feel every inch of it but felt weirdly immobilized, as if drugged, and unable to wake myself up and stop it. My initial thought was that it was some kind of horrific nightmare and I had imagined the whole thing. Only this is not something you imagine or make up. The evidence of the rape showed itself when I landed in the emergency room a few months later as the result of an untreated pelvic infection. Horrified and slowly grasping that my biological father had somehow drugged me and terribly violated me, I found myself bound to silence and incapable of telling doctors, family and friends what had really happened.

As expected, I spiraled into a serious psychological and spiritual aftermath. My behavior spun out of control with drugs and alcohol, boyfriends, rage and rebellion. I had also become physically ill with the onset of a sleep disorder, something that affected my school attendance and grades. In addition, I felt encased in a tangible darkness and was being actively tormented by demons. As for the Mormon church? I had failed their religious standards, and they clearly had no power to help me heal. A few years later and in complete desperation, I attended a small Pentecostal church service at the invitation of a relative. There I encountered the felt presence of Jesus Christ and gave my life to Him. I was also filled with the Holy Spirit, with the evidence of speaking in other tongues.[1] The total experience silenced my rebellious behavior and brought a radical turnaround. I began my new life absolutely in love with Jesus Christ, after being filled with the power of the Spirit.

In contrast, my biological father left the country shortly after he sexually assaulted me and eventually reemerged in Japan. He no longer held any employment that I knew of and appeared to be starting a new life as well, a life which included a young Japanese girlfriend. I do not recall who told me this, but I was keenly aware of his deep affection for East Asian people and culture in general. Although I am unclear on the exact details, he did migrate back to the United States after being hit and injured by a large vehicle while walking the streets of Japan. He was later found dead in his apartment, supposedly from "too much alcohol consumption." When

I received communication about his death, I was a junior at Oral Roberts University and studying mass media communications. My first reaction was a feeling of deep relief. I did stay in communication with my grandmother as she grieved her dead son, but I did not attend his funeral, and I never explained why.

I believe now that my biological father's passion for the Orient was most likely a missed spiritual assignment. In his unbelief and ungodliness, he never engaged that assignment for the Lord. Still, Jesus does not forget nor revoke what He has purposed us to do. We read in Romans 11:29, "For the gifts and the calling of God are irrevocable," and this was something the guest prophet was pointing to by the unction of the Spirit.

To illustrate, the first generation of Israelites came out of Egypt with a sure promise to have their own land, only they forfeited their spiritual inheritance because they did not believe it. The blessing of land did not evaporate like their faith did and was handed down to the next generation instead. You probably know the story from the book of Joshua, that Joshua led the next generation of Israelites into their blessing and they received their spiritual inheritance. I, too, was the next generation, being given an inheritance forfeited by the previous generation.

"The ministry that was on your father is now coming onto you," the prophet had said. The good thing is that Christian counseling had served to bring me to a good place to process these memories constructively when they surfaced. The prophetic word did take some time to process, but I was able to work through it and see the redemption of the Lord. Once this prophetic word was spoken, several East Asian ministers at the conference began to flock all around me while handing me their business cards. Within a year, I began leading intercessory trips into China.

Can you relate to this journey at all? Have there been deep battles in your family? I want you to consider what the war is really over. Spiritual inheritances and generational blessings come highly contested by Satan and his demons. These hideous battles have been sent to steal your bloodline blessings, yours and your physical and spiritual children. No matter how ugly your battle has been, I want to assure you that God is speaking a good word over you.[2]

An Unusual Resurrection

I was planning my fourth intercessory trip into China. An intercessory trip is similar to a short-term missions trip, but with a different objective. Instead of evangelizing and preaching, we arranged our travel to be in key areas needing intercession (i.e., Tiananmen Square,[3] Tianfu Square,[4] etc.). We were still invited to share the Gospel in some amazing places, but our main assignment was clear. We were to establish His Kingdom and His peace with our targeted intercession. Before traveling, we always prepared our hearts in fasting and prayer.

During one such time of prayer for China, the Holy Spirit spoke to me with unusual clarity. He said, *Don't go to China. Go to Thailand and intercede there.* By now, I had grown to really enjoy China: the busy city life of Beijing, the authentic Chinese cuisine, the beautiful terrain of Chengdu, its culture and its people. I was equally thrilled to be called to pray and minister in the unique spiritual terrain of Thailand.

I presumed it would be even more spiritually challenging, given its reputation for corruption, idolatry and sex trafficking. The Holy Spirit was entrusting me with another prayer assignment, something He does with His intercessors from time to time, and something I did not take lightly.

I did not have any ministry contacts inside of Thailand, but only God's clear directive. I did not know where to go in that nation or even what church to connect with. Based on previous prayer assignments, I still knew that everything would line up perfectly, and I took some bold steps without having everything in place. Prayerfully I selected a small team of intercessors to partner with. We then decided and announced our travel dates to our circles and waited for God's plan to unfold. Soon I received a message from a wonderful Christian businesswoman in Thailand who offered to help my team and me begin our prayer assignment in her country and in connection with her church. In addition, I received another invitation to minister at a prayer conference near Perth, Australia, right beforehand. I felt God's deep presence on that one as well. The Australian invitation was a little too perfect, to be honest. It promised to be pleasant weather and was located right near the Indian Ocean. Since I live and breathe prayer, I anticipated the Perth conference to be a more simple and relaxing assignment before the harder one in Thailand. I was completely wrong.

While in Thailand, we began our intercession in Bangkok on a busy city square that hosted a cluster of infamous shrines and idols.[5] These idols commanded worship from thousands upon thousands of followers, even around the globe. The spiritual atmosphere in the area was thick with demonic activity. The strongest and most discernable idol was the god of fortune, being represented by a large, gold Thai elephant. In the presence of this demonically charged idol and its worshipers, the hair on the back of my neck and arms would stand straight up on end. You could also feel a tangible anger emitting from the idol as if it had detected "trespassers," meaning worshipers of Jesus. After we interceded for the salvation of the people and for the geographical area, we proceeded to minister at a Christian business meeting later that evening. The people who attended came very well-dressed, wearing suits and ties, and were all very hungry for the Holy Spirit. They also received quite a bit of deliverance from spiritual oppression as you would expect, some even vomiting as their demons left them.

This level of intercession was difficult, but we hosted a tangible grace from God and walked in enough spiritual authority to navigate this climate without incident. Perth was surprisingly more difficult. One reason was due to an ancient demonic stronghold in the land, a kind that I had never encountered before. The term *stronghold* appears at least fifty times in the Bible. It often refers to a fortress that is hard to access (see Judges 6:2; 1 Samuel 23:14). A stronghold can be both natural and spiritual. The apostle Paul uses the term to describe a mindset or attitude:

> For though we walk in the flesh, we do not war according to the flesh. For the weapons of our warfare are not carnal but mighty in God for pulling down strongholds, casting down arguments and every high thing that exalts itself against the knowledge of God, bringing every thought into captivity to the obedience of Christ.
>
> 2 Corinthians 10:3–5

Consequently, I was not properly prepared to fight and overcome this stronghold and had to learn an entirely new area of deliverance.

What happened is I began to encounter an ancient snakelike deity revered by the Australian aboriginal tribes known as the Wagyl. I wrote about this journey in more detail in my book *Glory Carriers*.[6] In summary, it had both elements of a Leviathan spirit, the demonic king of pride[7] and a python spirit, which is a spirit of divination.[8] The spiritual attack came a few weeks prior to the trip in the form of a respiratory illness that made it very difficult to breathe and forced an unexpected trip to a hospital emergency room and then five days of bed rest. An attack on your breathing can point to the presence of a python spirit, which acts like a natural python attempting to suffocate you to death. Sadly, I lost relationship with three close ministry partners all around the same time to that wicked demon of pride. The Leviathan nature of this territorial spirit was that strong.

I have learned over the years that the greater the attack, the greater the reward. We prayed and interceded through all of this and learned much along the way. We still made it to the prayer conference, and it proved to be very powerful ministry. What awakened the meat of this book, however, was the outflow of an unusual encounter with the Holy Spirit that took place the last night after the conference.

I was sound asleep in my room and was awakened by the Holy Spirit in the middle of the night. He pulled me out of my bed in a very beautiful and tender embrace. I would describe His presence as liquid love being poured all over my entire being. Upon contact, something from Him dropped into my heart, and my heart was suddenly resurrected. Until that moment, I was not aware that half of my heart had died in some kind of an emotional death. The dead part of me came back to life in the most unusual and sovereign way. The encounter was so obviously life changing that I ministered out of that experience for a solid year with many similar testimonies from those whose hearts revived as well.

Why does your heart die like that? I had said that my heart died because of "life," which is true. I had said that I deadened my heart subconsciously to remove the pain of life's betrayal, grief, disappointment, hurt and more. This was also the truth. Even more true was the seriously crazy and unbelievable issue that unfolded in my life, an issue that I did not know was there. It was so unbelievable I did not even know how to talk about it. It also required the ongoing help of inner healing and deliverance ministers, a professional Christian trauma counselor, trusted friends and account-ability partners—something I will describe more throughout the book. It went deep, and parts of our heart die off like that for a reason, but dead hearts really do come back to life.

A Prophetic Word about Restoration

A few years prior to my memories returning, the Holy Spirit began preparing me to walk through the most intense per-sonal season of inner healing and deliverance that I have ever experienced. His presence came upon me with repeated and strong thoughts about the "vindication of the Lord"[9] through this prophetic word:[10]

> To be vindicated is to be cleared of blame or suspicion and to be proven right. Like you, I have dealt with far too many

disappointments and injustices. Like you, I have had to surrender these complex situations to Jesus and trust Him completely for the outcome. What I heard in my heart were His clear plans to bring both you and me into His total vindication, restoration and [divine] recompense.

He next confirmed this to me right from the Scriptures, saying, "The LORD gives righteousness and justice to all who are treated unfairly" (Psalm 103:6 NLT).

Have you been treated unjustly? Have you done the right things, only to get the wrong things in return? Do you need to be vindicated?

Then receive this word:

1. *He's setting wrong things right.*

You've waited a long time for your breakthrough in that situation and in those relationships. You've cried, begged, forgave and refused to hate. You've prayed, fasted, shown kindness while being mistreated and were determined to keep a clean heart. He says, "I am setting wrong things right. I am melting hard hearts. It wasn't you they were fighting. They were fighting Me in you, but I will win that fight. I will capture their hearts, and in turn, bring you peace."

2. *He's making crooked things straight.*

There were some wrong paths, wrong decisions, wrong attitudes and wrong actions done not on your part, but on the part of others. These were the crooked set-ups that broke your heart, stole your peace and interfered with your life again and again. He spoke to my heart, "I am turning everything around for your good. I will create beauty from the ugly and hard situations. I will straighten everything out, smooth things over and set things back right."

3. *He's restoring, but with an exclamation point!*

I heard these words, "Reinstated and restored!" Dictionary .com breaks down the word *restore* as "being brought back, put back, and given back." You are being brought back into your excellent condition. You are being restored to your rank. You are being given back what was stolen. You are being repaired and renovated in such a way that makes a clear statement to your doubters, mockers, and enemies. You are being reinstated. Honor is being returned to you.

4. *He will pay you back and pay you back double.*

There are many of you who have obeyed the Lord and did not deviate under pressure. You stayed in the assignment He called you to. Still you were persecuted, treated unfairly, dishonored, and experienced loss. You've had a Joseph experience [deep betrayal], a Job experience [Satan stole everything] and a Daniel experience [falsely accused and punished], yet you've remained steadfast in the waiting. The Lord's firm promise to you is this:[11]

- Double honor for your shame;
- Double possessions for what was stolen;
- A double portion anointing; and
- Twice as much as before.[12]

In the Bible, we learn about Job, who was "the greatest of all the people of the East" (Job 1:3). He was blameless, upright and feared the Lord. He was wealthy and blessed of God. And then, in one day, he lost everything, including his ten children. These were not natural circumstances either. Job was in a spiritual battle. Satan was competing against God for the loyalty of Job's heart, but God was confident Job would stay loyal to Him, which is exactly what happened. Job did not curse the Lord in his terrible affliction and remained faithful to Him. How did God repay Job? He gave him twice as much as he had before (see Job 42:10). Job also had ten more children.

My point is the Lord does not forget the faithful. "To the faithful, He gives double recompense. He will make a table for you in the presence of your enemies. He will show you off and pay you back! He will pay you back double!"[13] You will have an inheritance to give to the next generation.

MY **PRAYER** FOR YOU

Heavenly Father, in the name of Jesus, I ask You to hover over and prepare the heart of each person reading this book. They have a heart journey up ahead, one they cannot take without Your love and words of encouragement coming forth at each step. Allow this book to be a light in the dark and a guide in the rough places. Allow my testimony of freedom to be a prophecy to these dear ones that You are faithful and will do it again in them. In Jesus' name, Amen.

KINGDOM REFLECTIONS

1. Spiritual inheritances and generational blessings come highly contested by Satan and his demons.
2. No matter how ugly your battles have been, God continues to speak a good word over you.
3. God will restore you and recompense you. He will pay you back double.

4. The greater the attack, the greater the reward. The Lord does not forget the faithful.

5. Dead hearts really do come back to life.

KINGDOM QUESTIONS

1. Have there been deep battles in your family? What did these battles look like?

2. Have you considered that battles in your family are demonic battles to steal spiritual inheritances? Do you know what that inheritance looks like?

3. How have you experienced the Lord's vindication in your life? Do you need to experience it more?

4. Has your heart shut down to shut off pain?

5. What emotions are you experiencing as a result of reading this chapter? How can you express them (e.g., by talking to someone you trust or journaling)?

3

Hearts of Stone

Early one morning, I watched in dismay as a small mouse scurried across the floor as I sat at the kitchen table drinking a cup of coffee. I found out later that my significantly younger half sister had adopted a pet mouse and had neglected to tell the family. She had hidden it in her bedroom, and it had escaped. When I saw it, I had an immediate and emotionally driven reaction. Instinctively, without thinking, I pulled my feet off the floor and up to the seat of the chair in a self-protective posture. My reaction made little sense. What exactly was the mouse going to do to me? Was it going to turn around and attack my feet in a frenzy? Of course not.

Some medical and psychological experts suggest we have two or more brains: our mind-brain, a heart-brain and some now say a gut-brain.[1] Without getting too clinical, most of us have noticed the contrast inside of us between our rational, logical thoughts and then our core feelings, beliefs and emotions.

Sitting in that kitchen, my emotions were in charge, and a childish belief still active in my heart came to the surface, namely that mice are scary and dangerous. But within a few minutes, my adult logic kicked in and began communicating the obvious back to my heart. *Hellooooo! Don't you know this is a small, harmless mouse?* My functional brain then gave the rest of me a directive: *Put your feet back on the ground and go get a mouse trap.* And that is exactly what I did.

The Bible says to "keep your heart with all diligence, for out of it spring the issues of life" (Proverbs 4:23). Another version reads, "Guard your heart above all else, for it determines the course of your life" (NLT). In short, whatever you believe deep down in your heart will come to the surface eventually—for better or for worse. My husband reflects that universal truth like this: "My heart will determine the borders and the parameters of my life." You might want to take a moment to say this out loud: "Whatever I believe in my heart is the way my life will go."

The Heart as the Center

When I talk about the heart, I am not talking about the heart as a vital organ, a muscle that pumps blood throughout the body. I am not talking about romance or romantic love either. The Bible mentions the human heart around eight or nine hundred times depending on the Bible translation. The *Vines Expository Dictionary of New Testament Words* defines the heart as "man's entire mental and moral activity, both the rational and the emotional elements. In other words, the word *heart* is used figuratively for the hidden springs of the personal life."[2] *Easton's Bible Dictionary* defines it as "the centre of spiritual activity," "the home of the personal life" and "the seat of the conscience."[3]

We have all sorts of belief structures tucked away in our heart that are reacting and resonating to things we encounter in our day-to-day life. They often make the first decision for us without consulting our intellect. Have you ever explored the origins of your likes and dislikes, fears, guilt or shame, reactions, obsessions and the like? We all have these hidden narratives whispering underneath our actions and activities. These nonsensical belief structures can also stay active, yet hidden for years, until something brings them to the surface.

A woman in one of my online mentoring groups expressed that she joined the group very intentionally for targeted personal growth. She then confessed that she began to struggle and sabotage herself in connection to our group almost instantly. In response to her post, I asked, "Is there a specific thought or emotion underneath your negative reactions?" Her summarized response was this: "I have a lot happening inside of me that I am not equipped to handle. It has me intimidated to even look at it." Her mind directed her to do something constructive, but her heart was not yet in agreement.

This can be crazy-making at times because you may perceive one reality in your mind, then react differently from your heart. And when our heart is wounded and beliefs have formed deep within that God never authored, you find yourself doing things you did not want to do.

When You Do What You Hate

The apostle Paul confessed, "In fact, I don't understand why I act the way I do. I don't do what I know is right. I do the things I hate" (Romans 7:15 CEV). Have you ever felt like the apostle Paul in this way? Maybe I am reading into this, but notice that Paul did not disclose his actions. He did not describe with any detail what was objectionable to his sense of right and wrong. I have often wondered if his conduct was not mentioned because it was highly offensive to his apostolic office. Whatever happened, he had observed a pattern of sin within himself that he could not always control, a pattern that led to his powerful exhortation to walk in the Spirit as a remedy to walking in the flesh. Paul continued, "There is therefore now no condemnation to those who are in Christ Jesus, who do not walk according to the flesh, but according to the Spirit" (Romans 8:1).

King David ran into something similar. He found himself in remorseful repentance after his adulterous affair with Bath-sheba, which resulted in her pregnancy. Going from bad to worse, he then orchestrated her husband's murder in an attempt to cover up his misdeeds. What David thought he could bury in secrecy was confronted prophetically by the prophet Nathan. In addition, their infant son became deathly sick, and David's sorrowful prayers for his son's life went ignored. What was David thinking when he did all of this? Maybe he was not thinking at all. David, in my estimation, was flowing uncontrollably in the direction and disposition of his own heart. He knew right from wrong but did the unthinkable anyway. Why?

We read David's heartfelt response to the Lord's rebuke in Psalm 51:1–2. He first asked the Lord for His mercy, and then to be washed clean of his transgressions, iniquity and sin: "Have mercy upon me, O God, according to Your loving-kindness; according to the multitude of Your tender mercies, blot out my transgressions. Wash me thoroughly from my iniquity, and cleanse me from my sin." Notice these three words being used in this psalm: *transgression, iniquity* and *sin*. They are similar, but with different meanings.[4] To sin is to miss the mark, like running a stop sign and doing so in the heat of the moment. To transgress is to cross a boundary line, such as going onto someone's property without their permission. Iniquity is also sin but sin that is premeditated and done on purpose. Iniquity is quite serious, as it carries the ability to travel through your bloodline. In other words, iniquity that you commit against the Lord will show up as predisposed behavior in your children and your children's children.[5] David brought his family iniquity, his predisposed behavior, before the Lord and said, "Behold, I was brought forth in iniquity, and in sin my mother conceived me" (verse 5). Many scholars suggest that David was conceived through an adulterous affair.[6] His father and mother committed the act of adultery, resulting in his conception, and David committed adultery, too.

David realized that something was deeply wrong within his own heart and asked the Lord for a work of creation. His desperate plea was this: "Create in me a clean heart, O God, and renew a right spirit within me." (verse 10 ESV). Simply put, David did not have the disposition of heart to walk uprightly. Commentators have written that "the word rendered 'create,' ברא berâ'" is used to described "the creative operation of God, bringing into being what did not exist before. . . . It is not the restoration of what was there before that he desires, but a radical change of heart and spirit."[7] This same Hebrew word for "create" also hints at something being cut with a knife, formed and shaped.[8] If you have ever experienced the "surgical knife" of the Holy Spirit, a supernatural experience where He cuts, carves and re-creates your heart to be more like Jesus, then you can relate to all of these descriptors.[9]

Who Do You Identify with More?

When I examine King David's failure story, I believe David had lingering issues with his identity. In his foundational core beliefs, was he a son of Jesse? Or was he a son of God? Was he an overlooked shepherd boy rejected by parents and held in contempt by his brothers?[10] Or was he God's chosen warrior king and divinely selected to lead the great nation of Israel? In order to lead and finish well, David had to identify as God's warrior king and a loved son of God far more than the rejected son of Jesse.

All of us desire identity with our family of origin. It is a familiar place, and there is a certain kind of security in familiarity, even if our family of origin is unhealthy. Could this be why God called Abram, a man destined to be the "father of faith,"[11] to first leave his family and country? "Now the LORD had said to Abram: 'Get out of your country, from your family and from your father's house, to a land that I will show you'" (Genesis 12:1). Would the blessings to follow have been forfeited if he had chosen to not uproot from the familiar in order to reorient into his new identity in God? "I will make you a great nation; I will bless you and make your name great; and you shall be a blessing. I will bless those who bless you, and I will curse him who curses you; and in you all the families of the earth shall be blessed" (verses 2–3).

Genetic ancestry testing is a popular way to discover the cumulative ethnicities that make up your bloodline. Many find an even greater sense of identity knowing they are 45 percent Arabic, 32 percent Italian, 8 percent Romanian, a hint Russian and more. This is a fictitious ethnicity composition of course, but if this were you, would you attempt to match your quirks and personality bents to any one of those nationalities? Most of us would, and naturally so. I know one woman who did genetic ancestry testing and reported she was matched to an old ruling family somewhere in Europe. She mentioned this to me more than once and with quite a bit of joy. Her birth family was a source of shame and pain for her, but her ancestry test revealed something much better. I believe this helped her to reorient her natural identity to something more positive.

The best news is that in Christ, we have all been made royalty and been given a new bloodline. "To Him who loved us and washed us from our sins in His own blood and has made us kings and priests to His God and Father, to Him be glory and dominion forever and ever. Amen" (Revelation 1:5–6). Here it is again: "You have made them a kingdom and priests to our God, and they shall reign on the earth" (5:10 ESV). Let this truth of royal identity sink down deeply inside of you. My prayer is that you will sense something transformational as you read over this, allowing God's words to penetrate the depths of your heart. You have been made a king and a priest by God, an identity that recalibrates your entire being.

When we neglect or fail to identify with this truth, we default into our old familiar heart patterns and sinful behaviors. I believe King David did just that. During the season when kings went out for war, for an unknown reason David stayed behind and sent his military commander, Joab, instead.[12] David was not doing what kings normally did, and it was during this season that David found Bathsheba and repeated the family iniquity.

We see another fallback pattern occur in the life of the apostle Peter. After he denied knowing Christ three times and just before He was crucified, Peter went back to the familiar fishing business, something he did prior to being called as a disciple. Remember that Jesus called him a "fisher of men" specifically and not a fisherman, but he went back to his familiar identity anyway and not his God-given one.[13] Does this pattern resonate with you at all? Have you, too, ever relapsed into your old unredeemed identity and its familiar, sinful ways?

One young man with a stunning photography gift shared how he was genuinely saved, water baptized and baptized in the Holy Spirit. He became disillusioned with "loveless and hypocritical church leaders" and fell away from Jesus and His Church to do whatever he wanted. "Satan got hold of my photography gift, and I began creating highly inappropriate imagery," he said. "But then the fear of the Lord came upon my life, and I began to respond to Him." One night he saw the plans of Satan to hijack his God-given ministry in a powerful trance. His reaction was a full detachment from all aspects of an unclean lifestyle. "I am now very aware of God's plans for my life," he added. "I haven't looked back since and am so grateful all this happened before it was too late."

In Ministry and Heartsick

For some, the patterned heart whispered silently for years and then finally rose up and ruined them. They did what they did not want to do and reached a point where they could not stop their uncharacteristically destructive and habitual behavior. Jesus said, "For out of the heart proceed evil thoughts, murders, adulteries, fornications, thefts, false witness, blasphemies. These are the things which defile a man" (Matthew 15:19–20). Nobody in their right mind, especially if you are in public ministry or public service, wants to fail like this. Like King David demonstrated, these kinds of things happen to the sick and unattended heart.

I recall one ministry wife who had an affair with a much younger man in the congregation; another who had an affair with both a husband and wife duo in their church and would not end it; others who fell into homosexuality; and then another who left her husband, a worship pastor, for a barely turned eighteen-year-old though she was near to being forty. All these women spoke in tongues and prophesied, and this is just a fraction of the stories I could tell you. Their collective behavior is horrific, devastating and hard to accept. With stories like these, it is easy to condemn God's Church as being rampant with sin and full of demonized people and leaders. That might be true, but underneath this problem are Christian leaders and Christ believers who are tremendously heartsick and in need of a new kind of heart revolution.

I have loosely referred to this pattern of ministry derailment as "pastor's wife syndrome." Generally speaking, it applies to the ministry wife who is vibrantly anointed, prophetic and presenting perfectly—that is, until about her fortieth birthday. Around that time frame comes a change—not really a change to her but a change to those around her. She stops playing the role and faking her presentation, something she has rehearsed internally for years. Typically, she goes back to the gym and starts doing things like CrossFit or training for distance runs. Her decision appears outwardly sound, but underneath there are hints of anger and independence attached to it. She then gets a secular job or starts a business to the applause of many, but a hidden drive for independence is the real motive. She had once been called by Jesus to the Church and to ministry alongside her husband. Somewhere in her journey, however, she forgot her God-given identity and lost all heart to continue in her calling.

Before you know it, she has filed for divorce from her pastor-husband because he is "controlling." She also turns up with a boyfriend, and not necessarily in that order. Her social media posts become less and less "Jesus-y" too, and soon she stops serving Jesus and His Church altogether. We scratch our heads in wonder, feeling either sad or critical toward her or both. Hiding her true heart condition, she avoids any real accountability. Nobody can say they really knew her, and she simply fades away right before our eyes.

I have learned that ministry wives are notorious for playing the part while not tending to their own hearts. Covering up their true pain, anger and disappointment, many have become skilled at pretending connection with people while being highly disconnected all at the same time. In this state, their hearts slowly divide between their inward heartsick reality and their outward ministry presentation. The truth is, a divided and sick heart cannot continue in supernatural ministry without some kind of breakdown. Without intervention and intentionality, this pattern and syndrome lead to toxic habits or derailment of the worst kind. It is an unavoidable collision.

If I had seen the self-destructive habits of ministry wives only a few times, I would not be writing about this dilemma. Sadly, I have watched several women in ministry follow most, if not all, of this patterned degeneration. Was it the devil attacking them? Was this spiritual warfare? I am sure Satan takes advantage of any opportunity to destroy ministers and their families. It also has to do with missing a key principle and theme hosted in the Bible—the instruction to take care of your heart. Perfectly presenting women, especially the churchy kind, are almost always hiding their true heart condition. Usually they implode or explode in some way at some point, often doing things we never thought they would do.

I have also known many Christian women and ministry wives who have hidden their heart sickness with toxic coping mechanisms. They are armed with fake smiles and white lies, secretly dependent on alcohol, struggling with bulimia[14] or borderline anorexia (and calling it "fasting"), sometimes cutting themselves to redirect the pain,[15] perpetually on antidepressants and prescription painkillers and doing just about anything to numb it all down.

I confirmed what I have encountered in others with a Christian physician. He responded out of his years of experience, "If their husbands and parishioners only knew . . ." He then mentioned a repeat experience and observation with women in ministry who have addictions. "I've observed them targeting gullible people in their congregations and craftily siphoning off prescription painkillers. When they couldn't connive any more pills out of their congregants, they would come to me demanding, even to the point of screaming, cussing and using the wildest manipulative behavior you can imagine."

Addiction turns good people into crazy ones, even the outwardly Goody Two-shoes women in Christian ministry. Realize that as disturbing as these behaviors appear, these are the toxic fruits of deep-seated roots and not the roots themselves. They exist because something in the heart is deeply sick. There is a cluster of foundational lies, childish rage, unresolved emotional wounds, complex trauma, deep shame, tons of pain and much, much more. Roots that bear bad fruit have to be uprooted. The good news is that we are promised perfect freedom in Christ, but our freedom begins with knowing our identity in Him.

Put an Ax to the Root

John the Baptist spoke to the unrepentant Pharisees, demanding that they "bear fruits worthy of repentance" and to quit claiming Abraham as their father since they did not act like him (Matthew 3:8). Biblical repentance means to turn away from something and return to God. It also means to change your mind.[16] He then said, "And even now the ax is laid to the root of the trees. Therefore every tree which does not bear good fruit is cut down and thrown into the fire" (verse 10). John was showing us exactly how to identify sin or the impact of others' sin in our lives and how to get rid of it. Bad fruit, or sinful attitudes and habits, always results from bad roots. Some examples of bad roots can be offense, bitterness, jealousy, covetousness, fear, pride, rage, lust, etc. To understand this better, contrast bad fruit with the good fruit of the Holy Spirit: "love, joy, peace, patience, kindness, goodness, faithfulness, gentleness, self-control" (Galatians 5:22–23 ESV). Whenever we exhibit bad fruit, we are admonished to go on a finder's mission to locate the root and discover how it got there. Now armed with understanding, we can make a decision to engage in the process of repentance and thus begin the journey of laying an ax to it.

Some roots are easier to identify and resolve more than others. For example, I had noticed that I was avoiding someone because I was harboring offense at her mother. I had not fully forgiven the woman for the harm she caused me and held it against her daughter subconsciously. There was a belief, an inner vow, within my heart that paired like this: *Like mother, like daughter!* This belief, coupled with my unforgiveness, was the root to the fruit of my avoidance and rejection of someone. It did not take long to figure this out, but I still needed to resolve it.

Jesus told the story of the king who forgave the large debt of a servant, but in turn the servant did not forgive another of a much smaller debt. When the king heard it, he became angry and "turned him over to the jailers to be tortured, until he should repay all he owed" (Matthew 18:34 BSB). This is a stern warning to us to forgive others if we want to be forgiven and not come under torment. Once I saw what I was doing, I forgave the woman I was offended with and quit avoiding her daughter.

Other roots are much harder to identify. We notice the pattern of bad fruit but cannot find the root because it is buried too deeply. I was counseling a middle-aged woman in a prayer line somewhere in Australia. She requested prayer for her difficult marriage. I asked her a few questions, and she explained, "This is my third marriage, and it is heading the same direction as the others." When she said that, I knew what the root was. I then asked her about her earthly father, a relationship she described as "terrible and extremely hard." With that, I pointed her to a few Scriptures: "'Honor your father and mother,' which is the first commandment with promise: 'that it may be well with you and you may live long on the earth'" (Ephesians 6:2–3) and "Judge not, that you be not judged. For with what judgment you judge, you will be judged; and with the measure you use, it will be measured back to you" (Matthew 7:1–2). I said, "Your whole life has been on repeat because you hate your father. You are repeating that 'terrible and extremely hard' relationship in every man that you marry." She gave me one of those stares that people give when they see the truth of their life for the first time. This turned into some good tears and a time of heart-healing prayer. Now she had something tangible that she could identify and uproot with the help of the Holy Spirit and would hopefully see new fruit in her marriage.

The Invitation

The prophet Ezekiel articulated a transformational miracle coming to the hearts of the captives. He prophesied God's personal words, saying, "I will give you a new heart and put a new spirit within you; I will take the heart of stone out of your flesh and give you a heart of flesh" (Ezekiel 36:26). What does it mean to have a heart of stone? One commentary described it in this manner: "In the ancient world the heart was the center for volition and the intellectual catalyst for feeling and action. A 'heart of stone' implied inflexibility and willfulness."[17] Another characterized it as a "stubborn, senseless, untractable heart, that receives no kindly impressions from the word, providences, or Spirit of God in its ordinary operations and influences."[18]

I respect their scholarly comments as being accurate. I, too, would like to comment, but more from personal experience.

If I were to define a heart of stone from my own testimony, I would describe it as "unfeeling" and "darkened" on the inside. It is a state of the heart that feels hard and icy, and lacking in empathy. You do not feel, you do not cry and you do not care. We read in Ephesians 1:18 how the apostle Paul prayed for the eyes of our heart to become enlightened so we could discern spiritual realities.[19] We also read a description of those who are mature in the Lord. Mature believers can discern good and evil through their senses.[20] Finally, we read a prophetic warning concerning these last days: "And because lawlessness will abound, the love of many will grow cold" (Matthew 24:12).

In my case, my heart had experienced some kind of emotional death in response to complex trauma. What is crazy is that I did not know what had happened. To survive horrific situations, our mind will often hide memories we cannot accept or process and bury them deeply into our subconscious. Only these memories do not stay buried forever and will keep looking for a way to surface.[21] My subconscious response to a known psychological pattern was to harden my heart and turn everything off so as to not feel pain or deal with my issues. This is what was behind the growing blindness that I felt on the inside of me and the cause of my general inaccessibility to my own feelings.

You and I have been invited to love and worship the Lord with our whole heart, an invitation aimed at our entire inner world. "You shall love the LORD your God with all your heart and with all your soul and with all your might" (Deuteronomy 6:5 ESV). How then is it possible for us to love and serve the Lord wholeheartedly when our hearts are not whole but broken and shattered? We might be sincere in wanting to be wholehearted, but we will not be able to because we do not have the kind of heart to carry forth that command. Within this passage exists a beautiful, yet hidden, invitation from the Lord. He is inviting us to receive inner healing and deliverance for whatever stands in the way of you and me being wholehearted to the Lord.

MY **PRAYER** FOR YOU

Holy Spirit, in Your beautiful grace and love I invite You to come and be a constructive fruit inspector in the lives of my readers. Show them any gaps they have had with their kingly and priestly identity. Help them to see and identify roots bearing toxic fruit and then enable them to put an ax to whatever binds them. Deliver them from any addictions, food disorders, patterns of self-harm or sexual sin. Transform and heal any stony places in their hearts and give them tender, responsive hearts once again. In Jesus' name I pray, Amen.

KINGDOM REFLECTIONS

1. Whatever we believe in our hearts is the way our lives will go. Things will not stay buried or suppressed forever. Our true beliefs will eventually come to the surface.

2. There can be a division inside of us between our rational, logical thoughts and our core feelings, beliefs and emotions. We will know one reality in our mind, but then react to another reality from our heart.

3. When our heart is wounded and lies have formed deep within, we find ourselves doing things we did not want to do. Like the apostle Paul described, we can end up doing things that we hate.

4. Addictions, food disorders, patterns of self-harm, affairs, etc. are not roots, but fruits. We need to put an ax to the root with the help of the Holy Spirit. The fruits will then resolve accordingly.

5. We have been invited to love and worship the Lord with our whole heart, only we cannot worship wholeheartedly until our hearts are made whole. Our hearts can turn to stone, meaning darkened and unfeeling, and stony hearts need inner healing to worship the Lord wholly again.

KINGDOM QUESTIONS

1. We all have hidden narratives whispering underneath our actions and activities. Have you ever explored the origins of your likes and dislikes, fears, guilt of

shame, reactions, obsessions and the like? If so, what did you discover?

2. In what situations have you noticed your thoughts and your feelings to be incongruent (in other words, your mind thinks one direction and your heart feels another)?

3. Do you present yourself to people one way, but act and feel differently when they are not around?

4. Are you noticing any heart sickness in your life after reading this chapter? If yes, describe.

5. It is impossible to worship God wholeheartedly until your heart has been made whole. What is your response to this?

4

When You Hate Someone

As beautiful and transforming as my heart resurrection experience was, I began to wrestle hard with an emotion I could suppress and control previously—hatred. It was always there on some level, but good Christians, especially ones in full-time ministry, are not supposed to have lingering problems with hatred. I felt bad for having hateful feelings and kept going to the Lord like a broken record, expressing forgiveness and then asking for forgiveness in return. This long-standing emotion would rise to the surface, stronger at times than others, and keep wanting to have the same conversation.

My rational self would talk it back down, saying, *This is stupid and old and totally irrational.* My logical edge succeeded in pushing this emotion back for decades. Only it did not go away. Not only that, my hate started to take on an increasingly toxic sting to the point that finally I decided to get some help. The truth is, I hated someone—a woman connected to my biological father. And I had hated her for as long as I could remember.

One of my earliest memories as a four-year-old was screaming uncontrollably at this woman and saying just that: "I hate you!" Even as an adult, this emotion of hate had a strange intensity to it whenever it came up. Looking back, I think I was scared of what I really felt because of its intensity. I knew biblically that hatred is not an acceptable disposition of the heart, having heard all of the threatening sermons about what can happen to people who hate others and refuse to forgive from the heart. "But he who hates his brother is in darkness and walks in darkness, and does not know where he is going, because the darkness has blinded his eyes" (1 John 2:11). Also, "Anyone who hates a brother or sister is a murderer, and you know that no murderer has eternal life residing in him" (3:15 NIV). I kept thinking, *I shouldn't feel like this, and I shouldn't have this problem,* only I did have this problem, even on my best days. As a minister and a woman of God, I had judged myself harshly for not being capable of forgiving someone as the Bible instructs us. On top of it all, this was turning into a fierce internal wrestling match, and one that I was losing.

Upon referral from a friend, I made an appointment with an inner healing and deliverance minister to try to find some help. Even though it was an emotional situation, it felt strangely spiritual. As I said in the last chapter, wherever there are bad fruits, then we need to look for roots. Until the roots are exposed and dealt with, you cannot change the fruit. It is impossible. Some roots are buried very deep, and the Holy Spirit has to take you through a process of excavation. When we are ready to face it, He will find a way to bring the issue to our attention for our ultimate good and not to shame or condemn us. Remember, He is a healer.

The Difference between Hate, Rage and Anger

Merriam-Webster's defines *hate* as "intense hostility and aversion usually deriving from fear, anger, or sense of injury; extreme dislike or disgust."[1] There is a progression from anger into full-blown hatred. Hatred begins with the emotion of anger. Suppressed anger turns to rage, and rage turns to hatred.

When you are angry, it is an emotional response to what someone did. For example, someone cuts you off on the road and you respond with the angry blast of your car horn or, for some, with a universal hand gesture. It is temporary, a reaction in the moment, and it is over. The underlying emotion was probably a genuine fear of being in an accident, and anger took control of your fear and stabilized the situation. Or your employee neglected to handle an important task. That negligence, what he or she did, caused you to feel or respond with anger. Again, anger was the cover emotion for what you really felt. Perhaps you were frustrated at missing an important deadline, or you feared losing an important client due to their negligence, or something else. Anger can be constructive if you recognize it as an emotion alerting you to something that needs attention in your environment. In the case of the negligent employee, too many episodes of negligence and your subsequent anger responses would naturally lead to a change in the employee's environment.

Rage, by contrast, is suppressed, bottled-up anger that can gush out and be highly destructive. Rage is more dangerous than anger. It might express itself violently, both physically and verbally. Uncontained rage behaves in almost a primal fashion and causes you to react without considering the consequences. When you are in a fit of rage, you might attack a person physically, throw objects or destroy property. You might also abuse someone verbally. Rage can be turned inward and result in self-harming behavior. Rage is also damaging to your emotional well-being and your body. It pairs with insomnia, depression and anxiety. It also can lead to heart attacks, strokes and a weakened immune system.[2] I recall watching a fit of rage coming from a middle-aged man who performed social work at a local government-funded agency where I was employed for a season. Nobody knew exactly what triggered him, but suddenly he began throwing his papers and sharp desk objects. Next, he picked up his desktop computer monitor and threw it to the ground forcibly, causing it to shatter. After his uncontained fit of rage, we never saw him at the agency again.

When we talk about hatred, I have noticed how culturally and religiously programmed we are to not have, feel or admit our feelings of hatred unless it serves someone's agenda. Hatred is different from anger because it is not about what someone *did* but about who someone *is*. We are often conditioned to hate certain political parties, perceived enemy nations or various ideological "isms" that appear to threaten our economy and culture. In the United States, we are strongly persuaded not to hate other races or alternative sexual orientations. We can still become an object of hate when we do not agree with unbiblical sexual orientations, however. In churches, we are pushed to forgive and love our abusers instantly. And we are taught to drop all of our hate at the altar without any process. That method does not work. Forgiveness is a starting place, but you must have some process to overcome hatred fully. For the purposes of this book, I want to focus on hate on a more personal level, specifically on the progression from anger into hatred because you have experienced an injury.

Do Not Give the Devil a Foothold

Anger in and of itself is not wrong. To reiterate, anger also acts as an alarm system, alerting us when something inappropriate is happening to us so we can deal with our surroundings. In biblical accounts, we see there is room for righteous anger. The Old Testament portrays God's wrath at the unfaithfulness of His people (see Numbers 11:33; 21:5–6); the gospels chronicle how Jesus became angry at the money changers in the temple (see John 2:15–16). "And 'don't sin by letting anger control you,'" Paul instructed the Ephesians. "Don't let the sun go down while you are still angry, for anger gives a foothold to the devil" (Ephesians 4:26–27 NLT). But righteous anger will lead righteous people into redemptive action.

Hatred, on the other hand, has a fixation to it. When we do not or cannot process our emotions in a timely and constructive way, anger will sit and fester inside of us and then turn to rage, even taking on spiritual dimensions. This becomes the open invitation to the devil to begin sowing lies into our heart. When it comes to hatred, frequently you will hear how someone hated a person for a very long time. Over the course of this long-term fixation, typically the person who hates will wish for his or her enemy to be harmed, injured, dead or suffer some other form of punishment.

One young woman shared how her stepfather beat her and her brother often while growing up, even referring to them as "slaves and parasites." As a teenager and having no place to resolve her anger and rage, she then turned to satanism to try to find power and protection. She performed incantations and cast hexes and curses on her stepfather—and anyone else who got in her way, for that matter. She has since become a Christian and is still healing but no longer wants bad things to happen to her stepfather.

The Holy Spirit is our designated Counselor on the earth. "But the Counselor, the Holy Spirit, whom the Father will send in my name, he will teach you all things, and bring to your remembrance all that I have said to you" (John 14:26 RSV). The word used for "Counselor" in this passage is the Greek word *paraclete*,[3] which "has been variously translated as 'counselor,' 'advocate,' 'comforter,' 'intercessor,' 'strengthener,' and 'standby.' This promised advocate, or counselor, is the Holy Spirit."[4] In times of anger, the Holy Spirit is on standby to counsel us and comfort us. He also prays for us and advocates on our behalf. When we experience anger because we have been injured, He will counsel us and lead us into the best course of action.

Satan can also act as a counselor, but a destructive one. When anger sits in us, when we go to bed on it and do not resolve it, we begin to have thoughts and plans as to how to handle the person or persons who injured us. These thoughts are typically vengeful and destructive and always justify themselves. We might even mistake these plans for the counsel of the Holy Spirit. One minister confessed how he went on autopilot with his anger after being humiliated by someone. He said about the person who embarrassed him, "I was making devious plans to humiliate him back!" In His grace, God intervened in the life of this minister by sending a prophet with just one word from the Holy Spirit. The word was, "Repent." Immediately the minister was convicted in his heart and repented. He then made a decision to resolve his anger with the help of the Holy Spirit and not through vengeance.

Vengeance is reserved for God and God alone. "Beloved, do not avenge yourselves, but rather give place to wrath; for it is written, 'Vengeance is Mine, I will repay,' says the Lord" (Romans 12:19). Human wrath always carries a certain level of demonic partnership, thus the instruction to be "swift to hear, slow to speak, slow to wrath; for the wrath of man does not produce the righteousness of God" (James 1:19–20). When anger becomes rage and then turns to hate, it affects our entire world negatively and can be passed on to our children through the bloodline—that is, until someone puts an ax to it.

Hatred Sits in the Bloodline

I come from mostly European ancestry, predominately Scandinavian on the paternal side and English on the maternal. Our English family ancestry is tied to a key Separatist leader by the name of William Brewster around the time of the historical *Mayflower* voyages to America. Separatists were Christians who gathered independently of the Church of England in reaction to its corrupt political and religious practices.[5] Separatists believed that churches should gather and be formed by the leading of the Holy Spirit and not by man or by the state. Independent church gatherings were highly illegal in England and subject to much persecution, thus causing many adherents to flee for more tolerant lands. Having fled to Holland and intent on exposing the corrupt religious elite, William Brewster had book printing and press operations that served to ruin the Church of England's plans for America.[6] Our family tradition believed that Brewster, along with his wife and children, fled permanently from the English authorities as stowaways on the *Mayflower*. There is no historical evidence to support this "stowaway" claim, but we do know the Brewster family boarded the *Mayflower* and landed in Cape Cod, and he went on to become a religious leader in the Plymouth colony, as well as a high-level political advisor.

The reason I am sharing this with you is to give you the background for what happened to me while attending a large conference in California several years back. It was a charismatic-themed conference, yet all around the room were ministers in collars from England and specifically from the Anglican Church. I did not think anything about this until a few sessions into the conference. As I sat toward the front listening to the speaker, I began to notice something rising up within the frame of my own being very much against my own thought, care or will that began to speak with clarity—but it was not me. It said clearly and with force, *I hate Anglicans*. It then felt like the emotion of hatred coursed through me like blood going through my veins. At this point I felt like I was going to lose control of my own behavior and self, and quickly I reached out to my seatmate for help. She responded,

"You need to go and repent to one of those Anglicans and ask them to pray for you." I nodded in agreement and left my seat in search of a sympathetic Anglican.

I identified a pleasant-looking couple by their British accent and approached them toward the back of the conference room. I had no idea how to adequately explain what had taken place and spoke quite awkwardly while trusting the Holy Spirit for the outcome. "It's a long story," I began, "and it's very generational, but I hate Anglicans." They stared at me, not knowing where I was coming from or where this was leading. I added, "I didn't know I hated Anglicans until now, but either way I would like to repent for my hatred and ask you to forgive me and pray for me." With that, they received my repentance with kindness and voiced their forgiveness. They finalized everything by praying a prayer of blessing over me, and I had no more issues after.

Hatred is a destructive force in the here and now that can stay active in the bloodline for generations, both physically and spiritually. In the book of Genesis, we read how Abraham and Sarah received a prophetic word from God about a promised son. When time passed and Sarah failed to get pregnant, she found a surrogate for Abraham with whom he conceived a child, naming him Ishmael. This was not God's plan, however, and Abraham and Sarah eventually had their own son together and named him Isaac. When Ishmael began to show contempt toward Isaac, he and his mother were forced out of Abraham's home. Ishmael still became a powerful nation despite this hardship.

There are many that suggest that Ishmael's descendants (most likely Arabs and Middle Easterners) have continued their original contempt over the centuries and to this day toward Isaac's descendants, the Israelites, although some dispute this genealogy and claim.[7]

I lean toward the original contempt theory because I have experienced and observed how hatred travels through family bloodlines, giving an open invitation to the devil for spiritual oppression and ungodly behavior until someone takes spiritual authority over it and destroys it at the root.

Do you have unexplained bouts of hatred toward a group of people or a certain kind of person? If so, it could be generational hatred. It is wickedly spiritual, a door Satan uses to seize control of your life when opportunity presents itself. You will need to repent for bloodline hatred and command the devil to leave you and your bloodline for good. To help you, I have included a prayer of repentance for you to follow at the back of the book.

Hatred Leads to Deathful Thinking

In its most extreme expression, hatred can lead to murder. People who hate almost always have ideations of death toward the person or group of people they hate. The apostle John wrote, "Whoever hates his brother is a murderer, and you know that no murderer has eternal life abiding in him" (1 John 3:15). We also read how Jesus referred to Satan as being a murderer from the beginning.[8] When we have succumbed to hatred, it opens a door to a sinister demonic spirit of murder to fill our imagination with wicked thoughts of murder and death. Wishing someone's death is the unmistakable signal that there is a serious spiritual problem with hatred.

Diana, a professional therapist in one of my online mentoring groups, shared how she had fallen into an obsessive hatred toward her mother-in-law. She and her husband began dating in college, became married and had three children. She had noticed problems with his mother at the onset but did not recognize the severity until well into her marriage. "She was passive-aggressive and manipulative in how she excluded me," Diana said. "She would ignore me when we visited and rarely made eye contact. I also noticed several pictures around her house of my husband and our kids, but there were none of me." Diana added that her mother-in-law would lavish affection and attention on her husband and kids and then give her the cold shoulder. She also criticized how their children were being raised, which created arguments between her and her husband. Diana cannot remember what her mother-in-law said that triggered this, but she was pumping gas and daydreaming about harming her. "I wanted her fully out of my life because of the strife she had created in my marriage. It was paralyzing," Diana expressed. "I had been fixating and ruminating on how much I hated her for a few weeks. I knew I needed help when I overfilled my gas tank while daydreaming about hitting her with my car."

Diana is a therapist. She knows all about this and still fell into its trap because she was in denial of the severity of her own feelings. She explained how she had rationalized her bitter and hateful thoughts by putting everything on her mother-in-law and not owning her own wounds, pain and sinful responses. Once she saw her need for help, she chose to attend an inner healing and deliverance session. "I was in total despair," she explained. "It took me so long just to say the words 'I forgive' and to release her. I was ready to, but my lips felt paralyzed."

Hatred acts as a chain around the heart that is resolved only slowly, and not completely, one layer at a time. Personally, I have had to work very hard on this. For some, we choose hatred to feel power over a situation, only it is a demonic weapon that harms us more than it helps us in the end.

Keep Looking for Hidden Roots

The ministry of inner healing is "the process of dealing with the sinful reactions and false beliefs that get lodged in our hearts during the painful episodes of life."[9] When we become aware of such reactions and beliefs, we can present these things to the Holy Spirit and receive healing, closure and freedom in Him. Sometimes this happens in a private setting between just you and the Holy Spirit. Other times you may need the help of a trained inner healing and deliverance counselor who carries the wisdom, experience and anointing to heal the brokenhearted and set the captives free.[10]

Deliverance ministry is the process of casting out demons. I know many who engage in just deliverance ministry without any thought to inner healing ministry, but that is not a biblical model. We read this description: "How God anointed Jesus of Nazareth with the Holy Spirit and with power, who went about doing good and healing all who were oppressed by the devil, for God was with Him" (Acts 10:38). Demons come to oppress, harass and torment by looking for an open door. That open door can happen through sin, but it can also happen through some kind of emotional wound that needs to be healed. Until that wound is healed, the door remains open. You might cast out a demon successfully, but it will come back because the door is still open. Inner healing ministry serves to shut those doors.

It took some time to book an appointment with an inner healing and deliverance counselor. Keep in mind that the effective ones are often busy, and as with a good doctor, you might have to wait awhile to get in. Once I had that appointment, however, I was asked to fill out a general questionnaire and to explain my need for ministry. I was very concise and wrote, "I hate a particular woman and can't get over it." I was also asked to fill out a spiritual family tree and disclose as best that I knew what sins and strongholds appeared with each family member. Finally, I was informed of the cost of ministry, which is normal and much like you would expect if you were to see a good doctor or therapist. Inner healing and deliverance counselors do not work for free and usually devote themselves to this kind of ministry work full-time.

As I got closer to the appointment, about thirty days beforehand, I began to have a series of dreams. I began watching my own forgotten story in bits and pieces during the night. It was really shocking to me, as I did not have a grid for what I was seeing. Much like my biological father, this woman was also a pedophile and had sexually abused me. My mind had forgotten these horrific acts of abuse, but my heart had retained it. The prayer counselor had also received a word of knowledge from the Holy Spirit about the root of my hatred, and she confirmed what I had seen in my dreams. I wish healing went faster, but I did not get rid of my hate in that three-hour session. To be honest, nothing seemed real at first, only I had too much hatred in me for it not to be real. I knew I would need a special kind of therapist as a result and went searching for a Christian trauma counselor to pair with my inner healing and deliverance sessions.

I still did not see any victory over this hatred for close to three years, even after knowing the root of it. It was too strongly embedded into me. I had latched onto hatred as a young girl in order to feel power over a situation that rendered me powerless. And almost every day since, I wanted this person to die and get what she deserved. I also had natural concerns about what would happen to me if I gave up the fuel that hate provided. Would I lose my fire? Would I lose my edge? It sounds ridiculous, but when you are a public person, your audience relates to you a certain way, so I feared that a change in my personality would break my connection with my followers.

During a prayer session with this same prayer counselor, I had a vision from the Holy Spirit. I was finally able to see a road open within my own heart that led straight to Jesus. I finally understood in my heart that I did not have to hate anymore. My mind absolutely knew this, but God's healing had never dropped down into my little girl heart until then. My power comes from Jesus, and my fire does, too.

MY **PRAYER** FOR YOU

Holy Spirit, I pray for every person reading this chapter who is bound to hatred personally or generationally. I ask You to loosen the chains of hatred that have held tightly to their hearts and bloodline. I invite You to come and heal the deep wounds inside the hearts of Your sons and daughters, in their lives and in the lives of their ancestors. Enable them now, in this generation, to fully shut the door to hate and find true forgiveness by the power of Your grace. In Jesus' name, Amen.

KINGDOM REFLECTIONS

1. Hate is intense hostility and aversion usually deriving from fear, anger or sense of injury. It is extreme dislike or disgust.

2. There is a progression into the emotion of hatred. Hatred begins with anger. Suppressed anger turns to rage, and rage turns to hatred.

3. Hatred is different from anger because it is not about what someone did but about who someone is.

4. Hatred can be passed on to our children through the bloodline—that is, until someone puts an end to it through repentance for generational hatred.

5. Wishing someone's death is the unmistakable signal that there is a serious spiritual problem with hatred. Those bound to hate will need inner healing and deliverance ministry.

KINGDOM QUESTIONS

1. Have you ever struggled with hatred? If so, explain.

2. There is a progression from anger to rage and then rage to hatred. Can you explain how each one is different from the other?

3. What warnings does the Bible give us about how to handle anger properly (see Ephesians 4:26–27; Romans 12:19; James 1:19–20)?

4. Have you ever experienced or observed bloodline hatred? If so, describe.

5. Did you observe any roots of hatred being revealed to you as you read this chapter?

5

Traumatized and Shattered

(Content in this chapter is sensitive. Read with caution.)

I had just dropped off my son to a birthday party and was enjoying the quiet drive home down the long country road. While driving, suddenly I saw in my mind's eye a picture of my right hand wrapped in layers of white handfasting ribbons. I had never studied the purpose for handfasting ribbons before, but my spirit knew the facts immediately. I thought, *Wait. That's about a marriage, some kind of pagan marriage.* I was beginning to remember something I had buried in my subconscious. As the memories began flashing across my mind like single-image flash cards, I then asked the Lord and myself out loud what I thought was an insane question. My question was this: *Have I been married before?*

As I will explain later in this chapter, complex trauma survivors do not remember traumatic scenes in a timely way or in a complete and chronological manner. These memories come back when you can handle them, and they can come back as clusters of jagged pictures. This reflects the shattering of a person's mind when they go through severely traumatic experiences. The images that flashed across my mind one after the other were these:

- *I'm thirteen or fourteen years old.*
- *I'm inappropriately dressed.*
- *It's late at night. Midnight?*
- *A room with high ceilings and stained-glass windows.*
- *A side room with books on shelves, like a study.*
- *My bio father is there. He did this.*
- *A pagan priest dressed in black.*
- *Guests are goth, Hollywood types. All men and a woman.*
- *I'm in a rage and demonized.*
- *I'm being married to this guy?!*
- *I hate him. I'm in a panic.*
- *I'm bound, sealed, pledged ceremonially.*
- *There are spirits.*
- *My mind goes black. I can't remember past this.*

After these jagged memories came flooding back like picture flashes, I had a quick vision from the Holy Spirit. In the vision, I stood in the courts of heaven and demanded a "writ of divorce." I used that language specifically and to my best recollection, I have never used the word *writ* in my entire life. I know it is a word used in the Bible, but I never gave it a second thought until this experience. A writ is "an order issued by a legal authority with administrative or [juridical] powers, typically a court."[1] At the same time, I had not engaged in the "courts of heaven" teachings and methods that were circulating in many charismatic circles.[2] I do not have a problem with this popular teaching, but I already knew how to get my prayers answered. I did not need to seek out another method to find a greater breakthrough. Still, I was in a very real vision and standing in the courts of heaven making a legal demand for a divorce. I came out of that vision verbally breaking every curse I could think of, and my heart and mind were racing. As usual, I did not know how to think about this and was not sure if it was real.

I planned to have a conversation with my husband once I got home, but the shock of the memory was too heavy. When your memories come back, you feel the memory as if it just happened to you. It is like a time capsule buried inside your mind, and the shell of the capsule has decided to melt and expose its contents. With that, I chose to just sleep on it and make a decision the next day. That next morning, however, I was in the shower and getting ready for a prayer service. While showering, I began to shake badly and felt a piercing abdominal pain. Quickly I grabbed a towel and lay down on my bed while calling to my husband for help. He came and found me lying there as I described. I was screaming, then said, "My God! I've been married before! They made me marry that guy!"

After this took place, I contacted an inner healing and deliverance minister familiar with satanic ritual abuse (SRA). I wanted some kind of verification that these groups performed such ceremonial rituals. You need to do your research and test the spirits so you are not being led by false narratives or demonic delusions. At the same time, do not dismiss your recovered, hard-to-believe memories just because they are past your grid of reality. That is the constant battle with SRA. Your mind keeps rejecting what it needs to process in order to heal. The inner healing and deliverance minister that I mentioned did validate my experience, as these kinds of rituals do take place. Now I needed a plan to heal from the trauma and also receive deliverance ministry from everything that still bound me to this false marriage. You cannot ignore the spiritual side of this. If you were ritualistically bound to something or someone, even if it was against your will, it will keep its claim on you and your children until you break it off. For me, that involved some prayer ministry sessions. You also cannot ignore how this entangled you emotionally. Trauma damages your brain, but you *can* be healed. I then did several sessions with a professional Christian trauma counselor.

Understanding Trauma

"Trauma damages your brain," she explained. I was shocked to hear this from my own Christian trauma counselor, but her remarks explained my plethora of struggles connected to having complex trauma such as amnesia, dissociation,[3] PTSD (post-traumatic stress disorder), ADHD (attention deficit hyperactivity disorder) and more. That is a lot of labels, but I am so highly functional that most people have no idea these are my issues. Either way, I discovered plenty of trusted resources that not only supported her statement but also supported from clinical research and survivors' recovery stories what the Bible promises so clearly. In Christ, your mind can be renewed, and you will find rest for your soul.[4]

Trauma occurs when you have one or more distressing events that cause overwhelming amounts of stress, exceeding your ability to cope or integrate the emotions involved.[5] That is the standard definition. I define trauma more simply—as the feeling of being hit, crushed and smashed to pieces on the inside. Trauma might occur after you have experienced a physical accident, the unexpected loss of a loved one, a natural disaster or being the victim of a crime. Depending on the severity of the trauma and the makeup of the person, there can be a wide variety of reactions and symptoms. For example, a person involved in a car accident might relive the accident in his or her imagination and emotions after getting behind the wheel of a car. A victim of an assault might have nightmares and flashbacks of the incident for several months or years afterward and find it difficult to feel safe.

Not everyone who experiences a stressful event will develop symptoms of trauma. Some people with symptoms of trauma will resolve after a few weeks, while others will develop longer-lasting and more debilitating effects. When the trauma results from a single event and one that is lower on the spectrum of impact, most emotionally healthy people can overcome it on their own with the help of the Holy Spirit and by meditating on God's timeless promises. For others, they might overcome trauma with the help of supportive family and community or with the help of a trained therapist.

Trauma and PTSD go hand in hand.[6] PTSD is characterized by unusual anxiety, flashbacks, nightmares, hypervigilance and other symptoms. Persons with PTSD might become hypervigilant to avoid situations that trigger the emotional flashbacks they are prone to have, which would cause them to relive the traumatic situation emotionally. They also might scan their environments for any sign of danger constantly because they never feel safe. For some, this has severe effects on their physiological chemistry and puts them in a state of hyperarousal. Being in a constant state of alert often affects their ability to sleep. When they manage to fall asleep, typically they will have nightmares. Their bodies do not know how to relax, and their heart rate might remain unusually high all the time and never slow down.

There is also *complex trauma* (sometimes referred to as complex PTSD), which results from "chronic exposure to traumatic events over a period of months or even years," such as long-term childhood spiritual or sexual abuse, prolonged physical or emotional abuse, sex-trafficking situations, prisoner-of-war situations and torture.[7] The symptoms of complex PTSD include "significant challenges with regulating emotions, periods of amnesia or dissociation, difficulty in relationships, distorted perspective about the perpetrator, and feelings of guilt, shame or lack of self-worth."[8] Someone with complex PTSD may have "intrusive re-experiencing of the trauma, as in PTSD, but this is coupled with more extreme distortions of perspective, dissociation or more significant problems with emotional stability."[9]

What Does the Bible Say about Trauma?

Have you ever slammed your car door on your finger or dropped something heavy on your foot? *Ouch!* Your first reaction might be a swift, involuntary facial contortion in response to the pain followed by some type of physical movement to try to move the pain out of your body part somehow. Most likely your hand or foot healed up within a few days of the incident, but the feeling of having a part of you smashed or crushed is what I want to focus on. We experience a lot of hits just like this in life that bruise us internally and cause emotional pain for an hour or a day perhaps, but then it is over and we forget about it and move on. When something hits us that is extremely hard, is exceedingly heavy and manages to overwhelm our entire system, it is like having a part of ourselves crushed from the inside out.

For example, there was a young man who not only loved life and his family but was also a motorcycle enthusiast. He had a vibrant relationship with Jesus, attended church regularly and was married to a fantastic wife. One unfortunate day, and not for reasons of personal negligence, he spun into a guardrail along the busy freeway while riding his motorcycle. He had his helmet and protective gear on, but his head was still crushed upon impact. The destructive blow to just one part of his body killed him entirely. This story illustrates why we need to get all the inner healing, deliverance and trauma release that we can. You might be highly functional like I am, living an externally successful life, yet ignoring the trauma deep within you. That crushed part of you, however, can destroy all of you if you keep neglecting it and do not do something about it.

Marilyn Van Derber, Miss Colorado ('58) and Miss America ('59), television personality and author,[10] had a secret that she kept even from herself that forced her to pay attention when her daughter turned five years old: "Beginning with a state of physical paralysis, Marilyn began to break down, mentally and physically. She later realized that her daughter's age had instigated feelings about the abuse," which started when she, too, was five years old.[11] She was an incest survivor, raped over and over again by her prominent and affluent father between the ages of five and eighteen. She found out later that her sister had also been violated in the same manner. She had tried to survive it by ignoring her past, only it refused to be ignored. What had crushed her in her childhood years rose up and almost destroyed her entire adult life. Finally, she went public and received much support and then dedicated her life to help other survivors like herself.[12]

The good news is you can be healed. Jesus said, "The Spirit of the LORD is upon Me, because He has anointed Me to preach the gospel to the poor; He has sent Me to heal the brokenhearted" (Luke 4:18). The word translated as "heal" in this verse, the Greek word *aphiesi*, means "to *set free* or *loosen* from the harmful effects of a crushed and shattered life. In the *King James Version*, it is translated to 'heal,' but the Greek speaks of a 'release' from the detrimental effects of brokenness."[13] The word translated as "brokenhearted" in Luke 4:18 "is from the Greek word *tethrasamenous*, the perfect passive participle of *thrauo*," which describes "a person who has been shattered or fractured by life."[14] It is the picture of those whose lives have been continually split up in pieces and fragmented. Does this describe your family life and how you grew up? If your family was abusive, addicted or divided, this is a word that would depict the aftermath in your emotions from the shattered relationships you have most likely experienced.

We read references in the Bible of those who have suffered a crushed and broken spirit. I believe this is the equivalent of our modern term *trauma* and explains what it is like to be internally smashed, shattered, crushed and broken. Consider these verses:

- "The LORD is near to the brokenhearted and saves the crushed in spirit" (Psalm 34:18 ESV).
- "A joyful heart is good medicine, but a crushed spirit dries up the bones" (Proverbs 17:22 ESV).
- "A glad heart makes a cheerful face, but by sorrow of heart the spirit is crushed" (Proverbs 15:13 ESV).
- "A man's spirit will endure sickness, but a crushed spirit who can bear?" (Proverbs 18:14 ESV).
- "The tongue that heals is a tree of life, but a devious tongue breaks the spirit" (Proverbs 15:4 HCSB).

One of the consistent activities of the Lord throughout the Bible is to find and gather what has been scattered so He can bring it back together and make it whole again. He desires wholeness for us as individuals, as families and as nations. When the Israelites were "scattered," for example, He promised to find every last one of them no matter how far they were driven away and to restore them as one nation (Deuteronomy 30:3–4 MSG). When Jesus fed the multitude by miraculously multiplying the few loaves and fishes, He commanded His disciples to "gather up the fragments that remain, so that nothing is lost" (John 6:12). Finally, we read in the book of Amos the nature of a good shepherd. "Thus says the LORD: 'As a shepherd takes from the mouth of a lion two legs or a piece of an ear, so shall the children of Israel be taken out who dwell in Samaria'" (Amos 3:12).

He is compelled to find every fragment and piece, gather them and bring them back together whole—a basic human reaction when we encounter a jigsaw puzzle spread out in pieces across a table. You cannot help yourself but to search out the pieces and arrange them to fit their proper place. God sees you whole, even if you are presently scattered in pieces. Just like our natural response to a jigsaw puzzle, He is compelled to find every crushed, fragmented and shattered piece of you and restore it to its proper place.

Repressed Memories: Fact or Fiction?

I kept assuring myself that if I just keep sowing to my emotional health, then eventually I will get a harvest of healing.[15] I was hanging on to a biblical principle, the law of sowing and reaping, because therapy by now had become grueling. Sexual abuse from a female was a type of abuse that I did not have a grid for. It is not something that is talked about hardly anywhere, and so I felt alone in the struggle to close this old festering wound. It also surfaced an internal pain that I did not have words to describe. I knew I had to make a decision as to how I would manage that pain and wondered whether medication was the answer or not. I rarely take medication as a rule, but finding ways to cope constructively was becoming harder. I still chose not to medicate myself, even though the emotional pain was unbearable on far too many days. I know this kind of abuse does happen but never considered this to be a part of my history. All I knew was that I hated her deeply and did not know why until now.

Things went from bad to worse when I asked a question out loud to both me and my therapist. "I wonder why my bio father and this woman connected to him were both pedophiles?" When I verbalized this question, I began to have this imploding feeling. Something was really wrong, and I had just unlocked Pandora's box.

Slowly the glimpses of ghastly memories began to surface. These graphic memories involved the deep wickedness of organized satanism and sorcery, countless scenes of violence and ritual rape, even a ritual abuse/pedophile network in Hollywood, California, and it just kept going and going and going. No wonder I had buried it all in my subconscious. I could never wrap my mind around such horrific evil and what had been done to me by those who should have nurtured and protected me instead. Now, finally, I had some reference points for the shattered areas of my life that I could not find answers for.

When complex trauma victims begin to "remember," their memories typically do not surface cleanly or chronologically. They come out in small bursts, kind of like popcorn.[16] For example, I remembered these short bites of information over a period of several months, surfacing like a slow infection:

- *It is mostly dark in the room. Candles.*
- *Adults are chanting in a group.*
- *I am very young.*
- *There is a terrible blood sacrifice.*
- *I am being raped as a child in front of that group.*
- *I am getting lost somewhere in my head.*
- *I feel like I have died.*

- *I am leaving my body.*
- *There is no hope here.*

These are very short bursts of memory without too much detail. This cluster of memories that emerged did provide explanation of some family dynamics that never made any sense. I still cannot remember my exact age or even where this took place. I cannot remember the names or details of the people involved. I remember only one person who was there, and it was her.

These very short glimpses took me months to work through, and I had just barely scratched the surface. My identity and who I thought I was growing up was completely shattered. Each time I remembered another small detail, I would have an emotional knee-jerk reaction and want to throw myself out like the trash. I could not accept the information and questioned all the time if this was even real, which is a very normal response. At the same time, I had to make a daily, and sometimes a moment-to-moment, decision to "choose life."[17] Death appeared as the perfect escape from what felt like a never-ending nightmare; only Jesus defeated death at the cross, and emotionally I was to do the same.

To complicate things was a well-argued controversy in the medical community about recovered memories. Some have argued they are fake or had simply been suggested to an impressionable mind.[18] I am sure that someone somewhere faked their horror story for weird or selfish purposes, or a therapist somewhere suggested a horrific scenario to an impressionable patient who believed it and ran with it recklessly. For me, I would not know how to fake my story or how to manufacture my surplus of classic symptoms and textbook struggles. If this story had been suggested to me, I would have rejected it. It is too hard to believe, and I would never waste countless hours of time, energy and money spent on recovery. Diane Langberg, clergy and psychologist for trauma survivors, wrote, "Numerous studies have documented that it is rare for children or adults to lie about abuse. When victims do lie about abuse, they tend to lie to protect their offender, not to get him or her into trouble."[19]

In addition, there were the ignorant remarks of some well-known ministers who preach a message of denial and how you should forget your past and only look to Jesus and His future for you. For those of us who did not even remember our past until we were adults, those remarks are very callous and deny any process needed for healing. One wife and mother who survived severe physical and emotional neglect, in addition to sexual abuse, sought help from her pastor. The pastor denied her problem, pain and healing process by responding, "Shouldn't you be over this by now?" Faith in Jesus does not deny the pain but looks right at it, walks toward it and then moves through it with the help of the Holy Spirit. Diane Langberg also said, "We often seem to want people who have suffered terrible things to just 'get over it.' They cannot. Evil has real impact and does real damage."[20]

In the mess of all this, I did not lose my faith in God. I have seen Him work too powerfully in the past and knew He was my only answer. At the same time, I expressed every ounce of disappointment and anger that I had. I asked very hard questions. We are in a relationship with God, and honest, authentic dialogue is part of the healing process. It is healthy and normal to admit your anger, grief, sadness and disappointment and to wait for Him to respond. He did respond to my heart many times, and one very notable time He responded in a dream. I dreamed I was driving my black sports car down a lonely, isolated road late at night. I pulled over to the side of the road and in the moonlight, I began digging into the dirt with just my bare hands looking for something important that I had buried. A police officer suddenly appeared asking me if I was okay. I noticed he was an outstanding-looking man. He spoke with an assuring tone and said, "I am very confident in your situation." At this, I woke up knowing the identity of the police officer and felt a divine peace. It was Jesus. I have seen Him in dreams before, and He is always breathtaking.

This might have been a difficult section for you to read because maybe you, too, have complex trauma and my story is causing things to surface and finally become real for you. If this is you, I want you to read chapter 8 carefully (see the section entitled "Can You Recover?"). You will need to make a plan to heal and to live the very best life God intended for you to have. God has a way of working beauty into the vilest, ugliest situations. What He spoke to me in the dream, I believe He is now saying to you. He is confident in your situation and knows how to bring you back together. He is the Lord your Healer.

Do Not Spiritualize What Is Emotional

Haley, in only her second session of professional counseling, came into her therapist's office bandaged, bruised and with cuts everywhere. Her highly empathetic counselor, totally shocked and having to hold back tears at the sight of her, asked her to describe what happened. Haley was a

new Christian. She was overwhelmed with frequent flashbacks of childhood torture and nightmares, and she had
attempted suicide recently. A group of well-meaning women
in her church noticed her pain and reached out by offering
to pray for her healing. When one of the women detected
"demonic activity" and attempted to cast evil spirits out of
her through traditional deliverance prayer, Haley became
uncontrollably frightened.

Traditional deliverance prayer is when someone attempts
to expel a demon from a person. In a Christian context, the
prayer minister might lay his or her hand or hands on that
person and say, "I command every demon (or a particular
demon) to leave this person now in Jesus' name." Tragically,
immature or inexperienced deliverance ministers might yell
at or push the person or behave very forcefully, trying to make
this happen. When you know your true spiritual authority
in Christ, however, you do not have to force anything to be
effective.

Haley did not understand what these women in her church
were doing whatsoever. In desperation and blind panic, she
jumped up in a frantic attempt to run away from the situation. She also did not see the clear glass window right in
her path until she crashed through it. The window was completely shattered, much like Haley's life, and she ended up
being treated at a nearby hospital.[21]

Haley not only had PTSD (which included flashbacks and
nightmares) but was also a complex trauma survivor, having
experienced childhood spiritual and sexual abuse. There are
different categories of trauma, and I will address the differences in the next section. Inner healing and deliverance
ministers have been venturing into the conditions of trauma

and looking for effective models and methods to facilitate healing. Many have had a measure of success, but deficits and gaps remain across most of the spectrum of inner healing and deliverance methodology. When it comes to complex trauma, which is the deepest form of trauma, there is a tendency to spiritualize what is simultaneously emotional and physiological. This is because of a lack of clinical education and training. In Haley's case, this was not something that could be cured in a few prayer sessions.

In traditional deliverance, Haley's reactions would be interpreted as her being bound to a demonic spirit of fear or something else. This is based on 2 Timothy 1:7, which reads, "For God has not given us a spirit of fear, but of power and of love and of a sound mind." The ministers would then attempt to cast out a demon of fear in hopes she would have relief. Unfortunately, using a one-dimensional approach for deliverance ignores the entire physiological structure underneath her reactions.

Was Haley bound by a demonic spirit of fear? Definitely. She had also been hardwired in her heart and mind to always be afraid as a result of so much childhood abuse. This would cause her to overreact with irrational, childish fear whenever she was triggered by something in her environment. In her case, the traditional method of deliverance would not be a complete solution for her. It could be part of her overall healing plan but then engaged when she was ready and knew exactly what was being done and why. The deep physiological and historical roots of her fear, on the other hand, would have to be addressed by someone trained and knowledgeable in healing neurological damage associated with this kind of abuse, and this can be a much slower process.

These well-meaning church ladies did not understand even the first steps for healing complex trauma. They further injured Haley and her relationship with God's Church when they emotionally abandoned her because she was beyond their expertise. I believe the Holy Spirit wants to bring a much kinder solution to these complex cases and address the deficits that occur in both the clinical and spiritual models.

Missing Memories Resurface

Over the past two years, my missing memories reappeared gradually but with regularity. At first, I thought I was making everything up, which is a normal reaction. I slowly deduced that my appalling recollections might be legitimate, just knowing how averse I am to drama, attention-getting narratives and especially wasting time, money and mental energy in healing and therapy environments over something not factual. I was not the kind of person who would make up a crazy, made-for-the-movies kind of story, especially one that completely gutted me and then changed the course of my life.

As I sat in a Zoom session with an inner healing and deliverance minister last year, all she asked was this: "Were you part of some kind of network?" She was referring to something that would have been occultic and organized. When she said this, my vision began to blur and fade out to black, and then I passed out. My subconscious mind knew the truth, but I shut down in shock anyway. Obviously I did wake back up, and we closed out the session with some simple prayer. By now, I thought I had effectively prayed through and cut off everything occultic in my past (i.e., Mormonism,

Freemasonry, teenage experimentation, etc.,). Apparently there was more, a lot more.

The next morning as I sat in my car, I had the shocking feeling that my soul had split in half somehow on the inside. I do not know how to explain it any better than that. The half of me that split off was demanding that I return to Hollywood and restart my life over there. I could feel this strange knowledge bubbling up within as to where to go and whom to find and what I was to connect back into, and I had no idea where that knowledge came from. This experience was both psychological and the result of old programming, something commonly associated with ritual abuse. Of course, the grounded half of me—still full of the Holy Spirit, the Word of God and His wisdom—would not allow myself to take off foolishly and leave everything. Still, I started hearing eerie voices and seeing demonic spirits instantly, and it felt as if a rope was pulling me out of place and sending me back into something I must have belonged to, only I could not remember it. This "splitting" feeling lasted for only a few days, and thankfully I had people around me to pray me through it so I could settle down and figure out what had just happened.

To make things even stranger, over the next few weeks I began hearing in my mind a spell that must have been cast on me by someone connected to whatever this network possibly was. I would describe the experience as similar to hearing in your mind an old song that you used to listen to on the radio. This spell was very poetic and well-crafted in language, only it had been articulated and cast with the evil intention to stop me from remembering something that should not stay hidden. In His goodness, the Holy Spirit chose to surface something from my past that was still harming me today. Also, this was in addition to having dissociative amnesia, which again is normal for complex trauma survivors. When I heard this spell sounding off inside my mind, I knew to enforce what Jesus paid for on our behalf at the cross. Jesus broke and rescued us from every curse by becoming a curse for us, but Satan will still try to put evil curses on us regardless. We have to make spiritual injunctions when this happens. With that, I used my words to break the curse made against my mind and memories. We learn from several Scriptures that our words carry life or death and will cause things to happen (see Proverbs 18:21). I said this out loud before the Lord and to the spiritual realm, "I break the power of this spell made against my memories in the name of Jesus! Holy Spirit, come with Your glorious light and reveal what You need me to remember."

The Holy Spirit then spoke to my heart to bring this situation to the elders of our church and to get their prayer covering. In healthy churches, designated elders carry powerful delegated spiritual authority and have the capacity to provide effectual spiritual covering in various matters pertaining to the church. This would be similar to Moses calling forth the seventy elders at the instruction of the Lord to receive the same anointing he carried, so they could lead in the same authority as Moses led. This is one reason why we are instructed to go to the church elders when we are sick and in need of God's supernatural intervention. They carry unique spiritual authority and can anoint you with oil and lay their hands upon you. The Bible says their faith-filled prayers to God will heal you (see James 5:14). I followed the Holy Spirit's instruction because I knew I needed this kind of spiritual covering. Some things were going to get uncovered, and thankfully we had a strong eldership in place. This journey was getting really hard at this point, but I felt I was at a place of no return. I could only go forward and trust the Holy Spirit to lead me through successfully.

I could not believe what I was remembering over this past year. These chunks, glimpses and slivers of memories kept coming up, leaving me overwhelmed and feeling dirty, defiled, violated, like garbage and on and on. There is always sexual abuse in connection with satanism and sorcery. Always. As I said before, there are a variety of different circles within these occult-practicing groups, ranging from your neighborhood satanic coven to actual networks of wealthy professionals. My biological father associated with a network of men who had organized themselves into a system designed to feed their sick, ritualistic fetishes. They were both pedophiles and practicing occultists who worked or resided in and around Hollywood. I was forcibly prostituted and ritualized within this network as a young teenager by my biological father. I remember fancy cars and hotel rooms and being drugged out of my mind. I was also housed for a little while in a mansion somewhere in Southern California. This mansion was a designated space that served this network's penchant to ritualize and rape underage girls like me. It was a true house of horrors. The acts of rape and violence that took place in this environment went beyond description.

I am aware within myself that a lot more happened within this framework than I can consciously remember. For example, I cannot recall the names of my abusers or exact places. I do remember just parts of different scenes, but then my mind goes blank and I cannot remember past a certain point. This is what complex trauma is like and why you can feel very unsure whether your memories are real or not. I have learned that what is real will stay with you, and then you will experience all the emotions of the memory as if it just happened. All these glimpses and emotions have stayed with me, especially deep feelings of shame having been ritualized and trafficked at the wiles of my own father. I know logically it was not my fault, but somewhere, somehow you come to believe a lie deep down in your heart that it is.

I have said many times that I know how to heal, but this has gone beyond challenging and difficult. I have had to pioneer a path out of sexual shame in a way I have never seen modeled before. My first hurdle to overcome was feeling alone. To clarify, I did not feel abandoned by God and I also had a good support system. I just felt alone in my story. My husband reminded me of Elijah's complaint to the Lord when he said in his distress, "I'm the only one left!" (1 Kings 18:22 ISV). The Lord responded graciously to Elijah that He had preserved seven thousand others just like him. Elijah and these seven thousand others were not alone in their stories, only they had not found each other yet.

Prior to my memories returning, I defined myself to be a successful author and itinerant minister who loved Jesus, and a wife and mother of two amazing children. I had defined myself as an overcomer and believed I had dealt with the worst parts of my history. Now I have discovered I was pledged to Satan unwillingly, had been trafficked within one of Hollywood's notorious satanic systems and was then terrorized by my bio father's network of associates with sick ceremonies and ritual rape. As a result, sexual shame took on a whole new roar in my world. I did not know anyone living at my level of success who had their memories return in this manner and then overcame it.

My battles through recovered memories, occultic programming and sexual shame were fierce. It was very possible that I could spin out and become a casualty, meaning I could have had an ugly public failure. I had to educate and grant permission to all of my circles, including our church eldership, as to what to do if I lost my mind and did something unthinkable. I had a much better idea now why some people had failed so badly and publicly when they were in the prime of their life. Most likely, shame was unraveling them from their past, and they might not have dealt with it yet or even remembered it. With that, I told them they would have to come out with my story for me if it ever came to it.

My therapist emphasized what a miracle this was. "No one with your story has ever made it into my office," she said. "They end up on the streets or in special living environments. That's why I know God's hand is on you." I became even more determined to find a path out and perhaps provide a model for others who suddenly find themselves in the same mess as I did—especially those who are public figures, like me.

MY **PRAYER** FOR YOU

Holy Spirit, I pray for all those who identify with trauma and struggled through this chapter. Give them tremendous grace right now, especially those who were triggered and might be struggling to breathe or even think. Let Your embrace be felt, Your words of comfort be heard, and strengthen them now in their inner man. In the days to come, help them to secure a plan that brings healing and freedom from the pain and horror of their past. Give them wings to take flight far above the emotional chains that have grounded them until now. In Jesus' name, Amen.

KINGDOM REFLECTIONS

1. When it comes to complex trauma, which is the deepest form of trauma, there is a tendency to spiritualize what is simultaneously emotional and physiological. This is due to a lack of clinical education and training among most inner healing and deliverance ministers.

2. Complex trauma survivors are not delivered or healed in a few prayer sessions. It is a much slower process.

3. Trauma damages your brain, but your brain can be healed. In Christ, your mind can be renewed, and you will find rest for your soul.

4. Trauma and PTSD go hand in hand. PTSD is characterized by unusual anxiety, flashbacks, nightmares, hypervigilance and other symptoms.

5. Repressed or "recovered" memories are controversial, with arguments both for and against their validity. You will have to go with your own experience and

trust the Holy Spirit to guide you into all truth when dealing with any missing memories.

KINGDOM QUESTIONS

1. Have you ever experienced trauma? How did that come about?

2. What about complex trauma and PTSD, which is layered trauma? Do you have this in your life? If so, how would you describe it?

3. When it comes to inner healing and deliverance, complex trauma survivors need a different approach than traditional inner healing and deliverance models. How can we create a kinder and more effective ministry environment for those with complex trauma?

4. What does the Bible say about trauma? Can trauma be healed?

5. Have you or someone you know ever dealt with recovered memories? Was there any resolution?

6

Deliverance from Cults and Occult Practices

Estrella's paternal grandmother and father, and other family members, practiced *brujería* (witchcraft) and Santeria ("a religion . . . in which Yoruba deities are identified with Roman Catholic saints").[1] "My grandmother performed my dedication," she explained. "When she died, my baby picture was found on the altar in her room behind a book called *The Bible According to Satan*." Estrella has been through a lot of deliverance and still struggles with some health issues that have no explanation, something I have observed as a symptom of generational witchcraft, meaning witchcraft that has been practiced across generations. Thankfully she has been healed of scoliosis, cancer and paralysis, and she has nothing to do with the occult.

Debbie has a far different story. She knew and loved Jesus as a child and also had a prophetic gift, including the ability to see into the spiritual realm. Her church had forbidden the gifts of the Holy Spirit and therefore made no room for her God-given gifts to be expressed. In adulthood she became a professional psychic instead—that is, until she came to a large charismatic church and realized she had a prophetic gift from God that was in the Bible. Debbie now participates on the church prayer and prophetic teams, and she also serves as an inner healing and deliverance ministry counselor.

Finally, Taryn sought the ways of magic out of revenge and retaliation. Desiring more power, she joined a coven and was initiated into Wicca in South Africa. Wicca did not satisfy her desire, so she pursued the path of high magic and was on the verge of satanism when God intervened in her life with a prophetic word through a pastor at her friend's church. She gave her life to Christ and had to go through much inner healing and deliverance, beginning almost immediately.[2]

What Is the Occult?

The occult (from the Latin word *occultus*, "clandestine, hidden, secret") means "hidden" and generally refers to the pursuit of some kind of magic or secret supernatural knowledge or power.[3] Just as there are thousands of different Christian church denominations with differing beliefs and practices, there are just as many variations of the occult, and historically so. Some examples are *brujería*, necromancy, Santeria, satanism, shamanism, sorcery, spiritism, voodoo, wicca, witchcraft and many more. An occultist might practice magic, conduct various rituals, worship nature, celebrate uncommon holidays and summon the dead or other spirits either as an individual or in circles, orders and covens. There is a difference between a cult and practicing the occult, and both can range from engaging in physically harmless philosophies and activities to very dangerous ones depending on their core beliefs and practices. Just to clarify, these are all spiritually harmful practices, even if conducted for benevolent purposes.

A cult, which is different in structure, most commonly means a religious sect organized around a strong leader and requiring beliefs or commitments not typical of other related groups (i.e., Mormons, Jehovah Witnesses, the Church of Scientology, the Church of Satan, etc.).[4] There are many designated cults that claim to be Christian and even use the Bible to assert their preferred philosophy of religion and spirituality, only it is a false interpretation of the Bible that cites Scriptures out of context or incorporates other so-called inspired literature. Not all cults are physically dangerous. They are all deceptive, however, and hard-set on keeping people from knowing the truth of the Gospel of Jesus Christ.

This might be oversimplifying, but typically people engage in cults or occult practices for a handful of reasons:

1. Their immediate family is in a cult or conducts occult practices.
2. They have supernatural gifts of the Holy Spirit but are not received in Christian churches.
3. They want power for selfish reasons or in reaction to some kind of abuse.
4. They are just curious.

Both inner healing and deliverance are needed to experience freedom from the occult. When deliverance is ministered, it can be fairly systematic in my experience. It is not always that way, but usually it presents somewhat methodically and simplistically. Due to the nature of the occult, however, and how it operates spiritually, deliverance is something that must happen and not go ignored. Inner healing, on the other hand, can require quite a bit more energy and attention, but let's discuss deliverance first.

Where Does Deliverance Begin?

Jesus spoke to Nicodemus about his need to be born again so he could see the Kingdom of God. "'How can someone be born when they are old?" Nicodemus asked. "Surely they cannot enter a second time into their mother's womb to be born!'" (John 3:4 NIV). Jesus responded, "Very truly I tell you, no one can enter the kingdom of God unless they are born of water and the Spirit. Flesh gives birth to flesh, but the Spirit gives birth to spirit. You should not be surprised at my saying, 'You must be born again'" (verses 5–7 NIV).

The phrase *born again* means "born from above."[5] Nicodemus had a real need. He needed a change of his heart—a spiritual transformation. New birth, being born again, is an act of God in which eternal life is imparted to the person who believes. Sinners are spiritually "dead," but when they receive spiritual life through faith in Christ, the Bible compares it to rebirth. Only those who are born again have their sins forgiven and become children of God through trust in the name of Jesus Christ.[6]

This is where deliverance begins—at rebirth. Your spirit man becomes infilled by the Holy Spirit and thus possessed by the Spirit of God. At the same time, just because you have settled the destiny of your spirit man, there are agreements and covenants that need to be annulled and broken, or they will be pursued against you at some point by your spiritual enemies. I will use a few natural examples to explain how this works. If you become born again and have a warrant out for your arrest, that warrant does not go away because you gave your life to Jesus. The next time you encounter a police officer, chances are you will be arrested and sent to jail. Another example would involve your natural, earthly contracts. If you have a mortgage and still owe on it, the contract you signed and agreed to does not disappear because you have become born again. We understand this in natural terms, but too often believe something different happens when it comes to our agreements and covenants made with demons through our past occult activities and practices.

Delivered from a Spirit of Sorcery

I was delivered from a demon about a year after giving my life to Jesus. It was a very controversial situation given that my church did not believe that a real Christian could manifest demonically or even need deliverance for that matter. Their line of thinking was, *If that happened to you, then you must not have been saved in the first place.* I have shared my deliverance story many times and have written about it in a few of my previous books. For that reason, here is the short version to give you the context.

During my freshman year in college, I was encountered by the real Jesus in a very powerful, life-changing way while attending a Sunday morning Christian church service. I actually grew up in the Mormon church, also known as the

Latter-Day Saints (LDS),[7] but had stopped attending in the wake of severe personal and family issues. This Christian church was old-school Pentecostal in style, an expression radically opposite to the ultraquiet, highly subdued Sunday gatherings at the LDS Church. It was at this church service that I gave my life to Christ, and within moments I was also baptized in the Holy Spirit and received my prayer language.[8]

My first year in the Lord was absolutely heavenly. I had a deep sense of God's presence and felt Him leading my way. I had also found a small charismatic church to attend for a season. My spiritual walk noticeably changed, however, after receiving a supernatural warning from the Lord about my need to use my spiritual authority. I did not know what that meant at all, but I do know that He warned me appropriately ahead of time. One thing led to another, and during a prayer meeting about a year after my conversion to Christ, a woman said to me, "I see a spirit of sorcery standing over you." When she uttered her vision, something picked me up and threw me against the wall. I then went into a grand mal kind of demonic manifestation, which included violent shaking and demonic voices coming out of my mouth. Sadly, this prayer group was unable to bring me into deliverance, and my church just ignored my need for help because they could not explain my experience.

It was a terrible ordeal to be left on my own to just figure all of this out. I suffered spiritual torment for weeks, but the Holy Spirit did not forsake me. He taught me how to use my spiritual authority. When that demon showed up in my bedroom to torment me once again, the Holy Spirit prompted me to speak straight to it and say with authority, "I will not serve you. I will only serve the Lord Jesus Christ."

His anointing on my words broke the yoke, and I was never tormented by that demon again.

Christians and Demon Possession

Many people wonder, *Can a Christian be demon possessed?* The following is an excerpt from the appendix of my book *Seeing the Supernatural*:[9]

It is a huge myth to believe that Christians cannot be demonized. Notice, however, that I use the *demonized* and not the word *possessed*. This is where most of our confusion has come from. We have confused *possession* with *demonization*, and they are two different things.

The late Derek Prince explained his objection to the use of the description demon possessed in certain passages of the Bible, claiming it is a mistranslation, such as in this passage: "That evening after sunset the people brought to Jesus all the sick and demon-possessed" (Mark 1:32 NIV).

"The word *possessed* suggest ownership . . . by a demon," Prince said. "Now I don't believe that any born-again, sincere Christian can be owned by a demon . . . but the Greek word that's used can easily be, and should be, translated demonized."

He went on to explain that many born-again Christians are still demonized. He said there are areas in their personality where the Holy Spirit is not yet in complete control because there is a demon that has to be dealt with.[10] . . .

The question remains, then, how much of a Christian can a demon possibly possess? In examining this, we need to recognize that we are all made up of three parts: spirit, soul and body. When Jesus comes into your life, He comes into your spirit and takes up residence. Paul wrote to the Galatians, "I have been crucified with Christ and I no longer live, but Christ lives in me" (Galatians 2:20 NIV). I believe Charles H. Kraft, president and founder of Deep Healing Ministries, says it best, "A demon cannot live in the Christian's spirit—that is, the person's central core, the part that died when Adam sinned, because Jesus now lives there."

So, then, how does a person know if he or she is under the influence of demons or not? I admit discussions like this can make people doubt their spiritual condition if they are not strong in the written Word and do not know who they are in Christ. It can also leave us with the impression that deliverance from demons will always be a big fight. . . .

More often than not, I have known Christians to be delivered with minimal manifestation from spirits in their soul such as rejection, fear, self-hatred, lust, torment and so forth after they repent, renounce whatever it is, and command the spirit to go. If there is a manifestation, there might be a sigh, a cough, a shake or a twitch when the spirit leaves them, which is a signal that they are free of it. Still, there will be other believers who will have a much stronger manifestation, and we need to be prepared for that without making it a formula for deliverance.

As for me, my personal deliverance from a spirit of sorcery became the foundation for anointed deliverance ministry through my life for those bound by spiritual oppression. This anointing also undergirded a ministry for strategic warfare intercession, an intercession that brings deliverance to regions and nations.

Break Your Demonic Covenants

I have compiled a simple list of what generally needs to be repented of and renounced by those who have been in cults or involved in occult practices. This is the deliverance side needed to break free from the occult. Again, biblical repentance means to turn away from something and return to God. It also means to change your mind. To renounce something means to cast off, disown and refuse to further associate with it.[11] Keep in mind that there are many nuances that will need to be addressed as you engage in personal deliverance from the occult, but here is a general list to start off with:

1. If you were ritually dedicated to a cult or deity, then you have to undedicate yourself.

2. If you opened something up on yourself spiritually, then you have to close it (i.e., a portal, third eye, etc.).

3. If you made a binding covenant with a demon through a ritual or sacrifice, you have to break that covenant.

4. If you made a binding covenant with a person through an occult ritual or sacrifice, you have to break that covenant.

5. If a demon took ownership of you either by consent or by force through a ritual or sacrifice, you will have to revoke its ownership of you.

6. If a person took ownership of you either by consent or by force through a ritual or sacrifice, you will have to revoke their ownership of you.

7. If you cast a spell, placed a hex or put a curse on someone, you need to revoke it.

8. If you practiced soothsaying, divination or fortune-telling in any form, you need to repent and renounce it.

9. If you contacted the dead in any form or did any rituals on behalf of the dead, you need to repent and renounce it.

10. If you prayed to or bound yourself to your ancestors, you need to repent and renounce ancestral worship.

11. If you used any objects for the purposes of witch-craft, you need to destroy the objects if you still have them. This includes jewelry, books and literature.

12. If you used sorcery to shift your human shape (i.e., to an object or an animal), you need to repent and renounce it.

13. If you practiced astral projection ("the ability of a person's spirit to travel to distant places"),[12] you need to repent and renounce it.

There are multiple things that people need deliverance from in general, but not all spiritual problems are handled in the same exact manner. For example, deliverance from a spirit of pride[13] would be ministered to differently than deliverance from a spirit of infirmity.[14] Repenting from specific sins that opened the door to spiritual oppression and then forgiving people who have harmed you are the main tools that undergird a successful deliverance, but the roads through the various issues are not all the same. You will read and understand more about those differences in the coming chapters. When it comes to the occult, however, it seems to lay hold of people and their families through strong claims of ownership. It seizes control through dedications, covenants, unions and intentional bindings. This mimics God's deeply covenantal nature with His people, but for nefarious purposes.

An Unholy Counterfeit

To understand how occult claims and bindings work, you have to consider what it is counterfeiting. It deceptively parallels the marriage metaphor strongly engrained into the thinking of the Israelite nation in her relationship with God. God endeared Himself to Israel as a caretaking husband, but then pressed charges against her for widespread "prostitution" and "adultery" in committing idolatry against Him with other gods and demons.[15] The charges made against Israel plagued the nation's present-day inhabitants and afflicted her future generations as well.[16] Still, He promised to bring the entire nation of Israel and her children back to Himself, because she belonged to Him.[17] This marriage metaphor, actually a binding spiritual truth, is strongly mimicked by the occult and demons hosting its practices through human agents. These demons seek to own you through binding covenants, which also infers the ownership of your children and your children's children—that is, until someone does the work of deliverance. If you defy or leave your demonic covenant, the acting demons or their human agents will try to keep you by coercion or force or come back for you and your children at a later time. Deliverance, then, is how you engage a spiritual "divorce" with the spirits you got tied to by engaging in various occult practices in one form or another.

Many scholars describe the covenant at Mount Sinai (see Exodus 19–24) as the formal wedding between God and the Israelites. Here He invites the entire Israelite nation to draw near to His presence, which had covered the entire mountain, and then to hear His instructions and promises. "When the Bible mentions a covenant, it's referring to a strong, solemn agreement between two parties,"[18] in this case between God and the nation of Israel. To clarify, covenants join entities together in union, involve promises, involve families and bloodlines, have strong spiritual implications and are not easily broken.[19] The covenant made with Israel was a covenant with His presence and His commands and promises. It was an agreement that brought blessings to the Israelites when honored, but terrible repercussions when dishonored.

God, who created everything with a word and is the Word, made covenant with us through the same, His words. This is the spiritual law that demons use to keep you bound. To break your agreements with these spirits, therefore, you must use your words and state out loud what you are breaking away from.

In deliverance prayer from the occult, or for any issue, we always use the name of Jesus. As believers in Him, we have been given the right to use His name in prayer and to bring deliverance from demons. "In My name they will cast out demons" (Mark 16:17). There is power in His name.

> Therefore God also has highly exalted Him and given Him the name which is above every name, that at the name of Jesus every knee should bow, of those in heaven, and of those on earth, and of those under the earth, and that every tongue should confess that Jesus Christ is Lord, to the glory of God the Father.
>
> Philippians 2:9–11

Not only is there power in His name, but even the most resistant demons must obey His name when a child of God uses it.[20]

The following (also listed in the back of the book) is a simple but effective prayer of repentance and renunciation from the occult:

In the name of Jesus, I repent of any and all occult rituals made by me or my forefathers. I renounce all dedications made by me or my forefathers to cults, cult leaders and their demons. I break all ungodly and binding covenants associated with cults and occult practices, both to demons and human beings. I break every claim for my life or my family through demonic rituals, dedications and ungodly covenants. I fully dedicate myself and my family to the Lordship of Jesus Christ. Holy Spirit, I now invite You to come and be the ruling Spirit over my life and my family in Jesus' name.

As you say this prayer of repentance and renunciation, list to the best of your ability the specific practices, the specific cults, and the names of demons, deities and people you bound yourself to or your family bound themselves to. You might consider doing this with a mature Christian friend or Christian prayer counselor in case there is a manifestation that occurs with you personally or in your physical surroundings. For example, those breaking free from satanism have experienced objects supernaturally moving around their home or in their environment in manifestation. Others, such as myself, have experienced demons not wanting to release their claim and the spiritual warfare associated with that. If this happens, you need to commit yourself to working it through, all the way through, until freedom manifests, because it belongs to you in His name.

The following is a list of common occult practices:

- Astrology
- Chakra reading
- Channeling
- Charmary
- Clairvoyance
- Coffee grounds reading
- Divination
- Enchantments
- Extra-Sensory Perception (ESP)
- Fortune-telling
- Grave soaking
- Hexes
- Horoscopes
- Idol worship
- Incantations and spells
- Magic (all forms)
- Mediums
- Nature worship
- Necromancy
- Omens
- Ouija boards
- Palm reading
- Parapsychology
- Psychic readings
- Psychokinesis

- Reiki
- Sacrifices (all forms)
- Seances
- Sending energy
- Sorcery
- Spirit guides
- Taglocking
- Tarot cards
- Tea leaves reading
- Telepathy
- Transcendental meditation
- Witchcraft
- Wizardry
- Yoga

This prayer will get you started, but due to the nature of the occult, you will have to be as specific as you can. Inner healing from cults and occult practices is going to happen differently depending on the context of the cult and the experience of the individual. Cults thrive on control and use distinct mental and emotional tactics to retain control over their adherents. If this is you, healing from cult control will involve unraveling their distinct litany of lies that held your heart with the help of the Holy Spirit and ideally with the support of a stable community of friends or family. Some goals to have are forgiving those who controlled you and then forgiving yourself for allowing that control. Next would be learning how to have healthy boundaries so you can freely live out the purposes of God while taking your mind and life back.

Similarly, inner healing from occult practices will vary from person to person and have layers of complexity. For some, they engaged in occult practices because they were curious. Others did the same because they needed to feel powerful. If this is you, inner healing would address what drove your curiosity about the occult or what drove your need for spiritual power. Inner healing would then align your heart back to Jesus, the Source of all wonder and power. If you are a satanic ritual abuse survivor or know a survivor, read the help guide in appendix A.

Whenever we deal with inner healing and deliverance, there is always a push to free ourselves and others from what is commonly known as the Jezebel spirit. Except most people have been misinformed as to how this spirit operates and what freedom really looks like for those who have come under its influence. The next chapter will open your eyes to how this spirit really operates and explain why so many people have not yet overcome its wiles.

MY **PRAYER** FOR YOU

In the name of Jesus, I break every curse that has come upon you and your family through cult affiliation and occult practices. I destroy every demonic claim against your life and legacy and release you to enjoy the fullness of union with our Lord Jesus Christ. May the tangible presence of the Holy Spirit and God's holy angels surround you now in Jesus' mighty name, Amen.

KINGDOM REFLECTIONS

1. The occult, from the Latin word *occultus* ("clandestine, hidden, secret"), means "hidden" and generally refers to the pursuit of some kind of magic or secret supernatural knowledge or power.

2. There are thousands of variations of the occult and historically so. Some examples are wicca, shamanism, witchcraft, sorcery, necromancy, Santeria, *brujería*, voodoo, etc.

3. A cult, which is different in structure, most commonly means a religious sect organized around a strong leader and requiring beliefs or commitments not typical of other related groups.

4. People engage in cults and occult practices most often because their immediate family are involved that way, they have supernatural gifts of the Holy Spirit but are not received in Christian churches, they want power or they are just curious.

5. Both inner healing and deliverance are needed to experience freedom from cults and occult practices but will depend on context and the individual.

KINGDOM QUESTIONS

1. What is the difference between a cult and practicing the occult?

2. Have you or your family been involved in a cult or occult practices? If so, what was the motivation for doing so?

3. Have you ever considered that occult practices are spiritually binding contracts that have to be broken through deliverance prayer? What happens when they are not addressed and broken?

4. Did you see anything on the lists of occult practices still needing your attention? Will you repent and renounce these practices?

5. Why do we use the name of Jesus, especially in the context of breaking demonic claims to our lives through occult practices?

7

Healing the Jezebel-Afflicted Soul

Kailey was young, unusually prayerful and had a strong prophetic gift. She had also served as a strong volunteer leader within a vibrant campus ministry. "My ministry leaders were always upset with me," Kailey confided to her pastor's wife with tears rolling down her cheeks. "The students come to me for prayer and advice often. I think my leaders are concerned about my influence." Slowly her pastor's wife had brought her into her circle and was starting to mentor her. Over time, Kailey was given charge of intercessory prayer.

People continued to voice concerns about Kailey. They tried to be kind, but it was the same theme over and over again. Kailey was perceived as manipulative. She was thought to be spiritually and emotionally coercive as she recruited prayer leaders and would then use guilt to keep them from quitting. She often had accurate prophetic dreams and brought accusation against people more than once as a result. She was later discovered as presenting herself with spiritual authority that had not been given to her and had targeted those closest to her pastors with prayer and prophetic words so as to elevate her influence. When asked about these situations, she always had an airtight story: She was innocent, someone was jealous, it was not what it looked like or she did not say it the way they said she did.

Her pastor's wife and mentor believed she was mostly innocent but still immature in her leadership. She was unable to see through Kailey's deceit for a long time. When Kailey had an accident that triggered some emotional unrest, her mentor suggested she receive personal prayer ministry, as she appeared to be coming under spiritual oppression. Kailey resisted the idea, but her pastor's wife persisted. Finally, Kailey agreed to receive ministry but then gave the prayer minister such a hard time that it was not worth the effort. By now Kailey was accusing her pastor's wife of mistreating her, which forced a decision to release Kailey from ministry for a season of recovery. During that conversation, Kailey let slip how she had been recording all their conversations, not only with her mentor but with other leaders in the church, in secret. Upon her shocking admission, which was a veiled threat, Kailey was immediately dismissed from the fellowship. Sadly, her mentor realized way too late that Kailey had been operating under the influence of what is commonly known as a Jezebel spirit.

There is a lot of misunderstanding about the Jezebel spirit, and some even question whether there is such a spirit at all. As I said earlier, every demonic spirit presents itself differently and therefore needs to be handled differently. When it comes to the Jezebel spirit, I believe most of the Church has handled this spirit completely wrong.

Who Was Jezebel in the Bible?

There are two women named Jezebel in the Bible. One was an infamous queen in the Old Testament, and the other called herself a prophetess in the New Testament. Although some have questioned if the New Testament Jezebel was really named Jezebel or if her name was symbolic, it is still no coincidence that she appeared twice in the Bible and notoriously so.

Queen Jezebel's story is found in 1 and 2 Kings. She was a princess and the daughter of the king of Tyre and Sidon. Her father, Ethbaal, was a priest of Baal, an infamously cruel and revolting god whose worship involved the lewdest and most degrading sexual behavior you could imagine. Ahab, Israel's king, married Jezebel and then led the entire nation of Israel into the vile and repulsive worship of Baal.

Two incidents in the life of Jezebel serve to illustrate what is meant by the "Jezebel spirit." The first is her obsessive passion for domineering and controlling others, especially in the spiritual realm. When she became queen, she worked fervently to rid Israel of any and all traces of Yahweh worship. She commanded that all of God's prophets be executed, then replaced the altars of worship with those of Baal. Her strongest enemy was the prophet Elijah, who proposed a contest on Mount Carmel between the powers of Israel's God and the powers of Jezebel and the priests of Baal. Of course God won, but despite hearing of the mind-blowing powers of the Lord, Jezebel refused to repent and swore on her gods that she would chase down Elijah until he was dead. Her obstinate refusal to see and surrender to the power of the living God would lead her to a violent end ultimately.

The second incident involved a righteous man by the name of Naboth. King Ahab requested that Naboth sell his land to him, land that happened to be adjoined to the palace. Naboth refused and announced that to sell his inheritance would violate the Lord's command. While Ahab pouted and seethed on his bed over the situation, Jezebel took matters into her own hands. She proceeded to frame the innocent Naboth and had him stoned to death. Naboth's sons were also stoned to death so there would be no heirs, causing the land to revert to the possession of the king. Such a single-minded determination to have her way, no matter whom she destroyed in the process, is a characteristic of the Jezebel spirit.

We see another reference to Jezebel in the New Testament, who appeared to be influencing the church of Thyatira much in the same manner as the original one. This New Testament Jezebel was not some cosmic reincarnation of the first Jezebel, yet they were two different women who behaved eerily similar to one another. Jesus warns the church at Thyatira and declares that she is not to be tolerated. "Nevertheless I have a few things against you, because you allow that woman Jezebel, who calls herself a prophetess, to teach and seduce My servants to commit sexual immorality and eat things sacrificed to idols" (Revelation 2:20).

Whoever this woman was, just like the first Jezebel, she refused to repent of her immorality and her false teaching, and thus her fate was sealed. The Lord Jesus cast her onto a sick bed, along with those who committed idolatry with her. The end for those who succumb to a Jezebel spirit is the judgment of the Lord. With that, Jezebel has become a highly controversial reference point both spiritually and behaviorally ever since.

Is the Jezebel Spirit Real?

Every good woman has a control fit now and again. That does not make her a Jezebel. We have almost made that name, Jezebel, into some kind of Christian cussword to label women who are outspoken and carry some power and influence. At the same time, every pastor I know has dealt with two different kinds of women at least once during their time of ministry. One is a spiritual woman and an influencer, usually prophetic, but definitely maturing in her attitudes and agendas. People whisper under their breath that she is a Jezebel any time she makes a mistake, but she is not. She is just irritating to others as she grows in her leadership. The other is, you guessed it, a very real Jezebel who has all the attributes I mentioned but then rises up to damage the church and terrorize the pastor and the leadership. You need experience this only one time, and you will agree that the spirit of Jezebel is real and not a myth.

What underpins the reality of the Jezebel spirit is the active spiritual role and function of the spirit of Elijah. The prophet Elijah was a rival enemy to Queen Jezebel during their time on the earth, being zealous for the pure worship of Yahweh. Eventually he condemned her to death when he received a prophetic word of judgment from the Lord. "And concerning Jezebel the LORD also spoke, saying, 'The dogs shall eat Jezebel by the wall of Jezreel.' The dogs shall eat whoever belongs to Ahab and dies in the city, and the birds of the air shall eat whoever dies in the field" (1 Kings 21:23–24). What was prophesied came to pass. She was thrown down from her window to her death at the command of King Jehu, and the village dogs ate her entire corpse that day. What happened to Elijah next sets the stage to understand how an actual spirit of Jezebel continues to operate against the Lord and His people.

Elijah was the second human who was translated into heaven without experiencing death. Enoch was the first, but unlike Enoch, Elijah was observed physically going up to heaven in a whirlwind by a company of prophets, including Elisha, his successor.[1] What is interesting is how Queen Jezebel had cursed Elijah with certain death, only he never died.[2] Elijah was also given an assignment in the earth, one that would continue until the return of Christ. We read the prophetic utterance through the prophet Malachi:

> "Behold, I will send you Elijah the prophet before the coming of the great and dreadful day of the LORD. And he will turn the hearts of the fathers to the children, and the hearts of the children to their fathers, lest I come and strike the earth with a curse."
>
> Malachi 4:5–6

Based on this verse, many believe that Elijah has an ongoing assignment in the earth for restoration and specifically to restore and reconcile families. It is a mystery how this happens, but both Jews and Christians alike believe that the spirit of Elijah carries a powerfully redemptive role that is happening right now and will continue until Jesus returns.[3]

Conversely, Jezebel was never about family. She both coerced and demanded that God's people break their covenants with God and with each other and commit both physical and spiritual adultery. She was an agent against the sanctity and safety of adults and children. She hated male authority and only dominated. She never submitted. I believe there is such a spirit of Jezebel that is a demon, a kind of spirit principality, that functions in the earth as the antithesis of the spirit of Elijah. Although John does not use the term *Jezebel*, he wrote about the coming judgment of a spirit known as the great harlot:

> Then one of the seven angels who had the seven bowls came and talked with me, saying to me, "Come, I will show you the judgment of the great harlot who sits on many waters, with whom the kings of the earth committed fornication, and the inhabitants of the earth were made drunk with the wine of her fornication."
>
> Revelation 17:1–2

When you read the impact of this spirit and how it affects every nation, you will notice that it operates in the family of characteristics that we have commonly associated with the two females in the Bible named Jezebel. I think this is the stumbling point for some people about the existence of a Jezebel spirit because it is not stated specifically. It is something inferred and then something we have tried to define from a biblical perspective, mostly because we have encountered this persona in people over and over again.

"A Jezebel spirit is a celestial power that has worldwide influence," wrote John Paul Jackson in his book *Unmasking the Jezebel Spirit.* "It is a demonic power in the heavenly realm that transcends specific geographical boundaries and can affect nations."[4] Prophet and minister Curt Landry wrote, "There are numerous characteristics to this purely evil spirit, but most fall within these categories: deception, manipulation, control, insubordination, feigned repentance, sexual immorality, pride." He added, "Even though the Jezebel spirit is named after Queen Jezebel, it knows no gender. This means that this demonic spirit can influence both men and women. The same controlling, manipulative, seducing, and prideful characteristics manifest in men, just as they do in women."[5] If you have ever studied narcissist personality disorder, you will see many of these same characteristics: grandiosity, manipulation, arrogance, lack of empathy, intimidation and rage, chronic lying, etc.[6] If you have ever lived with or worked for a narcissist, you understand there are almost no words to describe how deeply manipulative and controlling they are. John Paul Jackson also asserted that even though it is a high-level spirit principality, the Jezebel spirit does not possess the individual in the same manner as other spirits do.[7] I have encountered the very same phenomenon and believe I can explain why.

A Nontraditional Possession

I shared this story in my book *Seeing the Supernatural* and for that reason will provide a condensed version just to give you context. During our first few years as senior pastors, there was a moral failure on our team. The circumstances of the affair were very hard to accept. The affair had also been masterminded by one of our worship leaders behind the scenes. This worship leader did not have the affair, but she had orchestrated it, believing it to be God's will. I was confused with her outrageous behavior because she appeared prayerful and prophetic, and she led worship from our platform. Over time, I did notice she was quite passive-aggressive and would apologize when confronted but never changed. I took note that both of her children had unusual issues with sexual sin and had been caught in acts of sexual defilement. Once her behavior was exposed, her family left our fellowship by necessity and then fell apart with divorce.

I began to study the common attributes of the Jezebel spirit and realized that she fit much of the classic description. For that reason, I washed my hands of her and never considered her worthy of redemption. I had judged her as too evil to ever change because, after all, she was a *Jezebel.* I had never considered God's heart for someone this sick and twisted inside. Later on, I began to wonder, *What causes someone to become that way? Can they change?* Many more women came through our church who fit the description of Jezebel, or they were somewhere within the spectrum of behavioral attributes. I had also noticed that we never could cast out a spirit of Jezebel successfully during deliverance sessions either. It was strange, because women would sometimes manifest demonically when this spirit was addressed, only it did not come out and they did not change either. That is how you know someone is delivered. They stop acting like the demon that possessed them.

With years of ministry under my belt and having dealt with several women who carried some or all of the attributes of a Jezebel spirit, I began to take note of their stories:

1. They hate authority, especially male authority. Why? Men in authority had abused them, often in the

worst way. To feel safe, they have to be in charge or control who is in charge.

2. In Christian churches, they gravitate toward the power dynamics of prayer and the prophetic. Why? They had suffered spiritual abuse by adults and authority figures. Having spiritual power over others is a much safer place for them.

3. They manipulate and seduce to get what they want. Why? Their needs were never met growing up. They had to hustle hard just to survive, even for basic needs such as food.

4. They are angry and intimidating. Why? Their power had been stripped from them, usually in childhood. They use anger and intimidation to survive a scary world where they never felt protected.

Without fail, it was always the same pattern—women with horrible stories who survived but then developed a personality reflecting some or all of the characteristics we commonly associate with the Jezebels in the Bible. I understood this dynamic intuitively, having fought so deeply with my own tendencies to use manipulation or intimidation to overpower people. My tendencies were ungodly and the fruit of inner vows that I made as a complex trauma survivor who did not want to be hurt anymore. It is subconscious and reactive, but these terrible survivor stories seemed to be a common denominator behind much of this kind of behavior.

Knowing this, we can understand better how the spirit of Jezebel gains control of its victims. This spirit principality unleashes sinister and targeted circumstances into a person's life to create the needed mental strongholds that result in the patterned behaviors. These targeted attacks can be childhood sexual or physical abuse, severe neglect, painful family issues and trauma, spiritual and ritual abuse and more. Not everyone with a difficult upbringing comes under the influence of Jezebel, but such trauma is intended to create its effects inside a person's heart and mind. When you encounter a person under the influence of Jezebel, realize that his or her wickedness today is a deep-seated response to traumatic conditioning yesterday.[8]

The Jezebel spirit does not possess people in the traditional way. Rather, it conditions them through trauma to transform into Jezebel inside their minds and personalities. This is the reason you cannot cast out this spirit—because people are not possessed by a Jezebel spirit; they actually *are* Jezebel. If you attempt to cast this spirit out, they still might manifest as if possessed by a demon due to the deep spiritual dimensions of this principality—only they do not change, no matter what manifestation you might encounter.

Remember Jesus' words about Jezebel:

> "Nevertheless, I have this against you: You tolerate that woman Jezebel, who calls herself a prophet. By her teaching she misleads my servants into sexual immorality and the eating of food sacrificed to idols. I have given her time to repent of her immorality, but she is unwilling. So I will cast her on a bed of suffering, and I will make those who commit adultery with her suffer intensely, unless they repent of her ways."
>
> Revelation 2:20–22 NIV

Here we see how Jesus dealt with her. He did not cast a spirit out but gave her the true remedy, which was repentance.

I have seen Jesus encounter such people in similar manner: He gives them time to repent before He removes them from harming His Church and His people any further. Some receive His warning and do whatever it takes to change their ways. Others refuse to repent and thus seal their fate.

I recall one young Christian woman who had been in foster care most of her childhood and suffered many things as a result. As a young adult and mother, she had developed many characteristics of the Jezebel personality and seemed to live a double life although she attended church regularly. In His goodness, Jesus intervened in her life supernaturally. During the ministry time at a conference that I spoke at, she received an unusual note posted to her cell phone. It frightened her, and she asked me and a few others what I thought about it. The note came onto her screen in big bold letters: "IN SIN." I knew her life well enough and by then had earned her permission to be honest with her. I told her this note came from the Holy Spirit and to be grateful for such a bold and supernatural confrontation. After this happened, she appeared to be making some progress toward positive change. That season did not last, however, and she reverted to making bad choices once again. She went on to become the mistress of a wealthy married man—that is, until he left his wife and married her instead.

Are you identifying with this personality? Do you have some or all of the attributes typically associated with a person under the influence of Jezebel? I have seen many of these attributes in myself, especially an unhealthy need for control. I say this from experience: As terrible as your past may have been, you cannot use your past as an excuse to continue in any one of these behaviors. You cannot continue controlling everyone and everything, manipulating, intimidating, lying, misusing prayer and prophecy, fornicating, dominating and refusing healthy authority in your life and then blame your sinful responses on your difficult past. Jesus paid the ultimate price to remove our sin, which means these things can be moved and set right within you. If this is you, realize that these behaviors were most likely your survival tools to survive the worst of the worst. Only now, your survival tools are working against you and against those around you. They are now the idols that Jesus wants to dismantle in your life so you can know His freedom and His blessings on an entirely new level. It is time to make an exchange, but to do so you will need to walk through the eye of the needle.

Through the Eye of the Needle

In three of the four gospels, Jesus gave a surprising response to the rich young ruler's inquiry, "Good Teacher, what shall I do that I may inherit eternal life?" (Mark 10:17). Since wealth was seen in the Jewish culture as proof of God's approval, the rabbis taught that rich people were blessed by God and were, therefore, the most likely candidates for heaven.[9] Jesus made it abundantly clear that nobody receives eternal life on his or her own merits and addressed the idol in the heart of the young ruler publicly. "Then Jesus, looking at him, loved him, and said to him, 'One thing you lack: Go your way, sell whatever you have and give to the poor, and you will have treasure in heaven; and come, take up the cross, and follow Me'" (verse 21). The ruler walked away very sorrowful because he could not part ways with his wealth. Jesus further explained to His disciples how hard it was for a wealthy person to inherit eternal life using this hyperbole: "It is easier for a camel to go through the eye of a needle than for a rich man to enter the kingdom of God" (verse 25). He was describing what level of miracle it would be for a wealthy person to worship and love Him more than earth's treasures.

How beautiful to know that Jesus specializes in transforming the hardest, most entangled heart into a true worshiper of Yahweh. When Jesus tells you that you can do something, it is because you can. You might need an absolute miracle to change, such as this rich young ruler did, but when He convicts you of sin, know that He will create a way out for you. When Jesus gave Jezebel time to repent of her misdeeds, it is because she was capable of changing. Even the most ingrained Jezebel-like behaviors are transformable in Christ and by the power of His Holy Spirit. If you think you are too damaged, are a lost cause and cannot change, I want you to think again. You are not too far gone. You can change, only it is going to take time, work and Holy Spirit power. It is a lifetime journey, but you will not be given a free pass to continue in Jezebel's ways because of your past.

I remember one young woman who struggled with anger and control. She was compelled to control her home and everyone in it. Her father was an alcoholic, and her mother enabled him while dominating his every move. She carried that power struggle and need for dominance straight into her marriage. When she punched her new husband while having a control fit, she learned instantly that he would not tolerate it. She was given the ultimatum right there to change her ways or lose her marriage. She decided to do the hard work and kept her marriage but failed to continue growing in other areas needing attention. She was an anointed teacher and had the Holy Spirit's gift of prophecy. In the church setting this was her sweet spot, but her tendency to become offended took her out of fellowship with God's Church. It was a terrible forfeiture and a reminder that we need to finish our race and not stop growing.

Another woman, who had been sexually abused by a close relative, carried her rage toward men into her marriage. Her husband was not as strong with her abuse as he needed to be. He had been seen multiple times with black eyes, facial bruises and scratches. Thankfully, her pastor did notice and confront the situation, insisting she get help for her rage and noticeable domestic violence. The problem in those with a deeply engrained Jezebel mindset is that real change can feel like an emotional death. Rage had become her core identity and not just a bad habit.

For as many women I know who did not overcome their Jezebel afflicted soul, I also know just as many who did and against all odds. Jayla is one such woman. She is still working her way out of this stronghold, but I believe she is on track to finish victoriously. Jayla was sexually abused by several people in her family and by people outside of her family. "I began to believe that I existed for just one reason, and that reason was perversion," she said. In her teen years, Jayla became increasingly aggressive in her lifestyle, and her mind was being bombarded with violent and sexually predatory thoughts. She also entered an abusive marriage but then fled the relationship after her husband almost killed her.

Jayla entered another relationship, and this time it was with a pastor. They lived together for several years, even ministered together, but were never married. "He was very perverse and didn't believe marriage was necessary," she explained. "We were also in a church where sexual sin was tolerated, even by the senior pastor." Jayla was preaching and teaching in this context. She was also addicted to pornography, something "women are not supposed to talk about." She added, "There is more grace for men coming out of this addiction, but there is not the same grace for women." The Holy Spirit spoke to her graciously to repent and come out of her lifestyle of sin.

Jayla clearly exhibited attributes we typically associate with Jezebel, only she did not do what Jezebel in the Bible did when confronted. She repented from the heart and began to study the Bible for herself and then take steps toward freedom. "I left that church and my lover, but was still addicted to porn," she said. "I went to a conference knowing prophetically that God was going to do something powerful in my life." And He did. At that conference, she was supernaturally delivered from a spirit of perversion, and her life completely changed.

Perversion, by the way, is one of the spirits that Jezebel will use to abuse and twist the minds of her victims. Although Jayla was delivered of it, that spirit tried to return, beginning with her thoughts. It was here she began to seek out inner healing. She needed to deal with the wounds, inner vows and generational sins that opened the door to her becoming bound by perversion in the first place. "I was birthed in an affair within a very incestuous family," she said. "Immorality, incest and rape were all around me, but I was going to be the one to break it."

Jayla is very strict in her lifestyle. She does not listen to music or TV with sexual overtones, and she avoids hanging out with people who carry that kind of spirit on them. She is determined to finish well and with purity. She has surrounded herself with people who are living right and attends a church that loves the Holy Spirit and practices the truths of the Bible. She was happy to step back into ministry, too. Remember that Jezebel called herself a prophet, but not Jayla. Instead, Jesus called her a prophet, and her church confirmed her call. She knows she has to keep growing and submitting to inner healing and deliverance on a regular basis if she is going to last. Still, her biggest battle was not with perversion and overcoming the Jezebel-afflicted soul. Her biggest battle was with shame, something that plagued her constantly and is the topic of the next chapter.

MY **PRAYER** FOR YOU

Heavenly Father, I pray for Your daughters and sons who have been targeted and traumatized by that sinister principality, Jezebel. I ask You to heal them from the horrors of their pasts through Your supernatural power. In the name of Jesus, I break off of them spirits of control, pride, rebellion, manipulation, rage and perversion. Give them the desire and the courage to conquer any behavior that looks like Jezebel and not Jesus. I ask You to uproot every evil root of Jezebel in their lives and strengthen them with might in their inner man by Your Holy Spirit that they not stop short but finish their race gloriously.

KINGDOM REFLECTIONS

1. There is a lot of misunderstanding about the Jezebel spirit, and some even question whether there is such a spirit at all.

2. What underpins the reality of the Jezebel spirit is the active spiritual role and function of the spirit of Elijah. Elijah was the second human who was translated into heaven without experiencing death. He was given an assignment in the earth to restore families, an assignment that would continue until the return of Christ (see Malachi 4:5–6).

3. A Jezebel spirit is a demonic power with worldwide influence. It transcends specific geographical boundaries and can affect nations.[10] It is the antithesis of the spirit of Elijah and works to dismantle families and covenant relationships.

4. There are numerous characteristics to this purely evil spirit, but most fall within these categories: manipulation, control, insubordination, feigned repentance, sexual immorality and pride. This demonic spirit can influence both men and women.[11]

5. The Jezebel spirit does not possess people in the traditional way. Rather, it conditions them through trauma to transform into Jezebel within their minds and personality. You cannot cast a Jezebel spirit out of a person because there is no spirit to cast out. They have actually become Jezebel.

KINGDOM QUESTIONS

1. How do you feel about those who are in authority, especially male authority? Do you find yourself able to submit to healthy authority, or do you fight and resist authority?

2. Do you gravitate toward prayer and prophetic communities? Do you pray or prophesy to truly serve God and others? Or does prayer and prophesying make you feel important and elevated?

3. Do you have a firm revelation that God will supply all your needs? Or do you manipulate people to get your needs met or to get what you want?

4. Generally speaking, do you feel safe and protected? Why or why not? How do you behave when you do not feel safe around someone or a group of people?

5. Do you identify with some or all of the attributes typically associated with a person under the influence of Jezebel? If so, are you ready for repentance and to begin the process of change?

8

Freedom from Shame

(Content in this chapter is sensitive. Read with caution.)

Jana had deep struggles with shame. For as long as she could remember, feelings of shame had overshadowed her like a cloud. "I would apologize for everything," she explained. "I would even apologize for my existence." During her childhood, she felt like everything was her fault and that she was the reason for every problem in their home. "I definitely believed I was a burden to my family and did not belong, although I could not explain why." Jana reacted to her negative emotions by trying to be the "good child" who did everything perfectly, only it never took the shame away. In high school, Jana sank into deep despair, anger and rebellion. "I abused alcohol and drugs and became very promiscuous," she said. "The men I slept with? I don't even remember their names." Jana had spiraled out of control, unable to receive love from anyone or allow herself to succeed. Eventually, she dropped out of high school.

Jana did get married but continued abusing drugs and alcohol. She also continued her promiscuous lifestyle through extramarital affairs. "When you are wrapped up in shame, it is a vicious cycle, and you perpetuate it with your behavior," she explained. Thankfully, the all-powerful Jesus had a much different plan for Jana. "I knew I was going straight to hell, but Jesus began a miracle in my life beginning with a dream." She further explained, "In the dream, Jesus called me to follow Him and to be in preaching ministry." As a result of this powerful dream, Jana gave her life to Christ wholeheartedly, then took the steps to become ordained in ministry. She remarked, "I knew with confidence that ministry was God's plan for me seeing His favor open all of the right doors." She shared how she was accepted into Bible school mysteriously without any transcripts, became ordained, served in multiple pastoral assignments and even taught the Bible at a ministry school.

There was a root to her shame, however. When Jana was thirteen years old, her neighbor spilled the beans and told her family secret—that Jana's mother had been in an incestuous relationship. "I was in shock," she exclaimed. "Was this really true?" Jana asked her mother the tough questions, and her mother confessed how she had been raped by her own father, Jana's grandfather, over and over since she was around three years old. She had also been brainwashed into believing her submission to his perverted advances would buy protection for her siblings, which was not true. Jana's mother had continued the incestuous relationship even after Jana was born, although Jana was not the result of their sexual union.

"I was in an inner healing and deliverance session when the Holy Spirit revealed a deep root to my shame," Jana expressed with both shock and gratitude. "He told me that my grandfather had threatened to take my life if my mother didn't abort me." Jana verified this revelation with her mother, who confirmed it to be true. This family secret was a deep root for her shame and, once discovered, became the catalyst for very real healing and freedom in Christ. She discovered that her grandfather had continued to threaten her mother with his plans to kill Jana after she was born, something her natural father confronted. Even though her natural father stepped in to protect her, shame had already firmly planted itself into Jana's young heart. To Jana's relief, her grandfather had later died of cancer.

"I finally forgave my grandfather," she said. "I realized I had made a lot of bad decisions in my life all because of shame." Jana shared that shame was a vicious cycle of self-hatred and condemnation, a true battle in the mind. She has been able to overcome her extreme thoughts and emotions by finding clear promises in God's Word. She explained her process like this: "I overcome shaming thoughts and toxic emotions in my mind by saying to myself my favorite promises in the Bible many times over. These promises center around God's full acceptance and deep love for me."

Jana had one last spiritual battle just after her mother died. She described how suddenly she was filled with sexually aggressive thoughts of the worst kind, and they came out of nowhere. She reached out for help and made an appointment to receive inner healing and deliverance ministry. "As I was prayed for, I saw in the spiritual realm a spirit that looked exactly like my grandfather and was clinging tightly to my back. I knew this was a familiar spirit,"[1] she explained. "I also saw the demon break off my back through the force of prayer. That is when the driving thoughts ended."

Jana wonders if she also inherited some of her struggles with shame through her own mother. "I suspect that shame is something that passes down from generation to generation, definitely in attitude and possibly in the bloodline. Either way, I'm putting a stop to it in my generation."

What Is Shame?

Shame is the internal pain we experience when we have measured our whole self to be flawed, bad or something to hide. This might happen after being humiliated by someone or in front of someone, after we have done something degrading or distasteful or when we have failed to live up to our own standards or the standards of other people. Shame is often confused with guilt, which is an emotion we might experience as the result of doing something wrong. The emotion of guilt will also cause us to feel remorse and have a desire to make amends. Whereas we tend to have an urge to admit our wrongdoing or talk with others about a situation that left us with guilty feelings, it is much less likely that we will broadcast our shame. We are more likely to conceal our feelings of shame because shame does not make a distinction between an action and self. With shame, therefore, "bad" behavior is not separate from a "bad" self as it is with guilt.[2]

One woman shared her struggle with shame after her husband left her for a mistress. "I'm remarried now, but my two children have different last names than my husband and me," she said. "I still feel a lot of shame about what happened to me and also to us." Another person shared her battle with shame after experiencing a devasting sexual assault. "Logically I knew it wasn't my fault, but I could not stop blaming myself," she explained. "I felt I should have been smart enough to see it coming."

I think we can all agree that shame can be a very painful emotion and not something we can always overcome logically. Just like all unhealthy emotions, there are different spectrums to shame, and unresolved shame can become toxic, even dangerous.

Shame becomes toxic usually after chronic or intense experiences of shame in childhood. Parents can transfer their shame to their children unintentionally through verbal messages or nonverbal behavior. For example, a child might feel unloved in reaction to a parent's depression, indifference, absence or irritability, or feel inadequate due to a parent's competitiveness or overcorrecting behavior.

> If not healed, toxic shame can lead to aggression, depression, eating disorders, PTSD, and addiction. It generates low self-esteem, anxiety, irrational guilt, perfectionism, and codependency, and it limits our ability to enjoy satisfying relationships and professional success.[3]

Toxic shame can also emerge from situations experienced in adulthood and drive people to start making bad decisions in life if they are not healed. People can no longer feel worthy or good enough after an experience causes them to see themselves as permanently stained, shamed and reduced in the eyes of others.

One woman became the talk of the town after her husband, who portrayed himself as a wealthy philanthropist, ended up in prison for extensive fraud. She has had a terrible battle with shame ever since and has struggled to maintain her spiritual and emotional stability. Another situation involved a minister following a strange mishap that occurred on a flight. Various newspapers alleged he had drunk alcohol and took sleep medication together and then fell into a deep sleep on a flight. While asleep, he had a dream he was using the restroom, but he urinated on a female passenger sitting next to him. I only paid attention to the article because I knew who this minister was. Both situations were terrible episodes that resulted in feelings of shame and would be difficult to overcome even by healthy adults without a lot of intentionality.

Shame can become dangerous when it is not resolved. One popular minister who ran youth camps and did evangelistic outreaches in junior high and high schools all over the United States discovered that someone on his team had been molesting kids in his camps. The signs of abuse were all there and for years, but they had been overlooked and largely ignored by this minister for an unknown reason. When victims came forward and the sexual abuse went public, this minister went into a posture of toxic shame. He did not overcome it and shot himself to death, leaving behind his wife and family. This is the extreme of toxic shame, but people can go there when they lack the skills and intentionality to resolve their extreme emotions.

What God Says about Shame

When Adam and Eve sinned against God, their perfect and beautiful covering of glory vanished. Some have suggested that Adam and Eve were clothed with God's glorious light instead of with natural clothing.[4] "Yet you made them only a little lower than God and crowned them with glory and honor" (Psalm 8:5 NLT). The Hebrew word for "crowned" in this passage can mean "to surround"[5] and "to encircle (for . . . protection)."[6] I believe this to mean that Adam and Eve were covered and clothed with God's glory, given they were encircled in His brilliant light.

After Adam and Eve violated God's command to "not eat from the tree of the knowledge of good and evil, for when you eat from it you will certainly die" (Genesis 2:17 NIV), their lives changed drastically. All of a sudden, they were barraged with difficult emotions, and the kind they had never experienced before—confusion, sorrow, guilt, horror, frustration and especially shame. They had damaged themselves, their environment and all of their offspring to come. Nothing would ever be the same again. Shame then awakened a human reaction in Adam and Eve, one we are familiar with now. Because of shame, they were strongly compelled to hide. "And they heard the sound of the LORD God walking in the garden in the cool of the day, and Adam and his wife hid themselves from the presence of the LORD God among the trees of the garden" (3:8). This is what shame does. It causes you to hide from people and especially from God. You feel unworthy of attention, love, forgiveness, being heard or even acknowledged. If you allow it, shame will isolate you and put you into emotional solitary confinement.

For the first time in their existence, Adam and Eve felt uncovered, exposed and vulnerable. Their eyes, and now their understanding, had been awakened, and they saw their nakedness. So they created a makeshift covering for themselves by sewing fig leaves together, which may have covered their physical bodies, but did not cover their shame.

> Then the LORD God called to Adam and said to him, "Where are you?"
>
> So he said, "I heard Your voice in the garden, and I was afraid because I was naked; and I hid myself."
>
> And He said, "Who told you that you were naked? Have you eaten from the tree of which I commanded you that you should not eat?"
>
> Then the man said, "The woman whom You gave to be with me, she gave me of the tree, and I ate."
>
> Genesis 3:9–13

As Adam blamed Eve, and Eve blamed the serpent for their sin, God acted to find a more suitable covering, one that pointed prophetically to a day when they could be free from shame permanently. He then shed the blood of some animals and made tunics for Adam and Eve from their skins. It was subtle, but it was a timeless statement that showed them what a sacrifice could do. A sacrifice would cover them, and they could stop hiding from the presence of God. Here we learn that God is the One who clothes us, covers us and removes our shame.

I believe God knew beforehand that we would suffer with horrible amounts of shame as fallen human beings, and for every reason you can think of. I also believe Satan orchestrates circumstances to try to bring shame upon you, but why? If you suffer with shame, think deeply about the following questions:

1. Why would Satan go out of his way to get you to hide because of shame?
2. Why are you such a threat to the kingdom of darkness that Satan has had to immobilize you with shame?
3. What would happen if you threw shame to the wayside and you were seen and heard for who you really are in God?

There is an empowerment from the Holy Spirit to walk out of shame. You were meant to be seen and heard, not hidden away in shame. Jesus took our shame upon Himself at the cross. He broke shame into pieces, then clothed us with His radiant glory once again. We have judged ourselves as shameful, yet He has crowned us, made us kings and priests, and shamelessly called us flawless (see Song of Songs 4:7; 5:2).

After interviewing dozens of people about shame and what caused shame to take root in their lives, there was one topic that came up in almost every conversation—sexual shame.

The Path Out of Sexual Shame

Despite the hypersexualized global culture we live in, sexuality seems to be an uncomfortable subject to discuss in most churches. Nor do we have safe zones in our churches for those discussions to even happen. Furthermore, when it is discussed, it seems like people do not have a clue as to how to respond or react, and they make it worse for people and not better.

I will give you an example of how ministers can make sexual shame worse and not better. In two separate conferences that I spoke at, a few of the other ministers began to call out a specific behavior being practiced by some of the attendees. Both ministers believed they had received a word of knowledge from the Holy Spirit about the sin of masturbation and needed to address it. A word of knowledge is one of the nine supernatural gifts of the Holy Spirit listed in 1 Corinthians 12:7–10. When this gift is in operation, the Holy Spirit will supernaturally reveal a fact about a person or group of people that is presently happening or had happened in the past.

Keep in mind that I am a prophet, but I am also pastoral. As a prophet I, too, get words of knowledge, but as a functioning pastor, I have learned that these "facts" do not always have to be said publicly or at all. Both ministers insisted that attendees currently struggling with masturbation either raise their hands to identify themselves or come to the front of the room and repent for it in front of everyone. I was horrified at their suggestion. I have pastored people through this issue before, and for some it is lust, but for others it is an entire root system that needs pastoral covering, confidentiality and space to heal. Telling impressionable people to stand in front of the room with cameras rolling was completely insane. It did not create any safety at all for these poor people to heal from their sexual shame. It only perpetuated it.

Sexual shame is a rampant issue in God's Church, and a very mishandled one. I believe it is due to unhealthy views about sexuality and then not knowing how to create safe zones for people to confidentially communicate their abuse, hang-ups and addictions. What I have learned over the years as a pastor and personally is that whatever the reason for sexual shame or shame in general, there is a path out. You can overcome this.

If you have generalized shame, sexual shame or toxic shame in your life, here are some steps to help you walk out of it:

1. *Break your silence.* Start with the safest, most confidential person you know and break your silence, even if this is a paid Christian counselor or inner healing and deliverance minister. Tell them what you can of your story. Right now, you are looking for people who will listen and simply validate your story. Every time you talk about it, the power of shame diminishes.

2. *Tell people what you need.* As a leader, I realized people did not know how to help me in the way I needed them to. They were used to me being emotionally strong and not needing much emotional support. I was also telling them things that had happened to me, one shocking thing after another, and giving them details they have never heard from anyone before. I had to be specific with those I included in my process and communicate how to really support me. All of my needs for emotional support were met, but I had to describe what that looked like to me.

3. *Create a support system.* No matter how strong and experienced you are as a leader, you will still need support to come out of any kind of deep shame. For me, it was counseling appointments, regular prayer ministry, personal prayer partners and trustworthy friends. I put circles and circles of safe people around me because I knew I was in a severe and very

complex battle and needed help. You might not need as much as I did, but you will need support.

Walking out of shame requires intentionality. The outstanding promises contained in God's Word can remedy every shameful situation we can think of. Shame is a fiercely emotional battle. And a spiritual one. You will need to exercise faith in God's promises and renew your mind to believe God's truths about you, for example, in Romans 10:17 ("so then faith comes by hearing, and hearing by the word of God") and Ephesians 4:23 ("be renewed in the spirit of your mind").

Can You Recover?

Last year, as I began to share more details of my story in a strategic way with people I worked with and ministered with, I took note of one woman's unexpected reaction. As I shared, I noticed how she appeared agitated and highly uncomfortable. She then asked if we could meet up afterward and we did. She had her own shocking story to share. "I just want someone to believe me," she explained. In the months after our conversation, she stepped into the whirlwind that every complex trauma survivor goes through when what you have worked very hard to ignore finally comes back and demands your attention. When these intense emotions hit, you always feel like you are too far gone and will never recover. You are not too far gone. You will recover, but you need a healing plan.

We are made up of three parts: spiritual, emotional and physical. Many of us understand that our physical health requires a plan. Physically healthy people will eat a certain diet, use supplements and incorporate regular exercise. Spiritual people, meaning believers in Jesus, also follow a plan for their spiritual health. They will read and memorize the Bible, pray consistently, fast on occasion and attend a healthy church. They will also seek out inner healing and deliverance ministry as appropriate for their needs. The same goes for our emotional health. You must have a plan to be healthy as well as to overcome the emotional cancers and emotional diseases that trauma survivors all carry. Emotional health is something that is largely overlooked in many Christian circles.

A *healing plan*, then, is the systematic structure that you construct around you to get well and to stay well. Nobody is going to do this for you. You have to create it yourself and then honor it. Here are some things that I do, but you will want to craft your own plan, something that is best suited to you:

- *Create an accountability group.* These are mature people you trust who will allow you to process your pain, encourage you and pray for you on a consistent basis.
- *Invite a few trusted friends into your process.* You might not want to share with everyone, but you need to share with someone.
- *Exercise.* This takes the edge off of highly intense emotions and keeps trauma from settling in your physical body and causing pain.[7] Recovery is very emotional. Exercise alleviates rage, depression, mental wars and a lot of other issues.
- *Routine.* This keeps you grounded, especially if you have problems with dissociation. When I prepare for a

ministry trip, for example, just the routine of packing my luggage in a predictable way is really therapeutic. When I am home, going to bed at the same time and getting up at the same time and doing mornings and evenings in a certain order seems to create peace.

- *Schedule things to look forward to.* These could include coffee dates, dinner dates, reading a good book, hikes, beach days, etc. It is a mental release just knowing you are going to do something you enjoy.

- *Find a Christian trauma counselor.* They have great tools to help you heal from the ravages of complex trauma. You might have to try a few out to find one that you like.

- *Get support.* Talk to a pastor or mature spiritual person regularly who believes in you, champions you and has faith for your recovery. Most of the time, you will need to initiate and schedule this conversation.

- *Receive ministry.* Seek out inner healing and deliverance ministry on a routine basis. There is a deeply spiritual side to complex trauma that has to be addressed, in addition to the emotional side.

- *Keep a journal.* This is where I write out my ugliest feelings and memories as a form of emotional release. Because I am a public figure, my journal is digital and with a password for privacy.

- *Have absolute faith in God.* If He raised Jesus from the dead, He will raise you up, too. Remember, this is a journey that takes time.

- *Be kind to yourself.* Have empathy for yourself. You will have bad days. Be good to yourself on those days and do not condemn yourself for not having it all together.

- *Make lists.* Have a list of things you will not let go of on your really bad days—things like God, His Church, your marriage, your home and family, your job, your life, etc. You will have seasons when you want to leave everything and even this world because of pain that is connected to your healing. You have to decide ahead of time what you will not let go of.

- *Rest in God's promises.* As emotional as this is, it is still a faith battle. I make it a habit to go back to His promises and take comfort in His promises to fully restore and heal me.

There really is something about putting your story in the light, but usually it is a slow process getting there. Sexual shame—or whatever kind of shame it is—will diminish once you have said your story to people who will not judge you or mishandle your information. You will have to find those people, and you will have to establish a structure around you to have those discussions, again and again, over a long period of time. You will also need to learn how to identify and overcome the spirit of fear, because it will try to start a conversation with you constantly.

MY **PRAYER** FOR YOU

Heavenly Father, I ask for an increased anointing to come upon the readers for freedom from the captivity of shame. Empower them to come out of hiding and to break their silence. Give them eyes to see themselves as You do, that they have been made flawless and are royalty. Even now, renew their minds to believe Your truths about them. You call them shameless! I pray they come in agreement with this truth and call themselves shameless, too. In Jesus' name, Amen.

KINGDOM REFLECTIONS

1. Shame is the internal pain we experience when we have measured our whole self to be flawed, bad or something to hide.

2. Shame is often confused with guilt, which is an emotion we might experience as the result of doing something wrong. With shame, however, "bad" behavior is not separate from a "bad" self.

3. Jesus took all our shame upon Himself at the cross and broke it to pieces. In Him, we have been crowned and made kings and priests; He calls us "flawless."

4. Breaking shame requires faith in God's promises. You renew your mind to believe God's truths about you.

5. To break shame, you will need to tell your story to people you can trust and create a support system to process and journey with.

KINGDOM QUESTIONS

1. Do you struggle with shame? Why or why not?

2. If you struggle with shame, has it become toxic? Dangerous? Do you need to get help now?

3. Satan orchestrates circumstances to try to bring shame upon you. Why would Satan use shame to get you to hide? Why are you such a threat to him?

4. What would happen if you threw shame to the wayside and were seen and heard for who you really are in God?

5. Sexual shame is very common, especially with Christians. If this is you, are you in a church that has safe places for you to work through sexual shame?

6. Many have a plan for their physical and spiritual health, but not for their emotional health. How do you stay healthy emotionally? Do you have or need a healing plan?

9

Defeating the Spirit of Fear

In 2014, I was ministering and teaching in Redding, California, about the gift of prophecy when I noticed a tall, slender woman with dark hair approaching me. My session had ended, and some attendees had come forward to where I was standing to ask questions or receive prayer. A line had formed in front of her, and she then sat casually on the platform nearby while I answered questions. I noticed out of the corner of my eye she had begun to shake physically. This was not too alarming, as people often shake in the presence of the Holy Spirit, and there was a clear sense of His presence in the room. She kept shaking, however, only it had become stronger and more violent. At this point, her shaking did not feel right with my spirit.[1] When I had a chance to talk with her, I first asked her for her name (let's just say her name was Helen) and whether she knew what was happening to her. Helen responded, "I feel crazy afraid right now, and I don't know why."

Typically, you can identify a demonic manifestation happening if you see someone growl, hiss, slither, scream unnaturally, roll his or her eyes to the back of the head, etc. At the same time, some people exhibit a manifestation, and you are unsure if it is the Holy Spirit or something else. They might fall to the floor suddenly or laugh in a very strange way. If you are unsure, you may ask them, and usually they can tell you. They will say, "It's God, it's demonic, or I don't know." If it is the Holy Spirit, you might just lay your hand on the person's arm, shoulder or head and say, "More, Lord!" If it is the last two responses, you will need to take authority over the demon and forbid it from manifesting any further if possible.

I always try to stop any demonic manifestations because the demon might throw or harm someone.[2] Just say, "In Jesus' name, I bind this spirit from manifesting in this person right now." You might need to say this two or three times before it stops, but then you can talk to the person more easily and investigate why he or she is manifesting a demon.

Helen knew what was happening to her. She said she was "crazy afraid," which meant to me that she had a spirit of fear and thus the violent shaking. We knew then what spirit it was, but now we needed to identify the reason, or the root cause, for why it had demonized her.

To find that out, ask a few questions such as, "Who or what hurt you and made you afraid?" Or, "When did you stop trusting?" Whatever the person tells you, that is your starting point for ministry. Remember to approach this as a process that could take time to work through and with the utmost kindness and patience, especially with complex trauma victims. Still, once they have forgiven their abuser or abusers, they will be set free from tormenting spirits more easily.[3]

In Helen's case, she did not know why she was suddenly afraid, so I just cast the demon out of her. I said, "In Jesus' name, I command the spirit of fear to leave Helen right now." She coughed and became rigid for a few moments, but then the spirit left her. The tangible peace of God came over her once the demon was expelled. By the way, all of this happened in fewer than ten minutes, and she left the room freer than when she walked in.

At another meeting, I had finished ministering before people had come forward to ask questions, receive prayer and socialize with one another. There was a young man standing by the podium about ten feet from me, conversing with another man. Like Helen he, too, began shaking violently, and this time I knew it was a demon. I walked over to him and asked, "Why are you shaking?" He said wide-eyed and desperately, "I'm not sure. I'm suddenly feeling an intense fear." In that moment, I received a word of knowledge from the Holy Spirit. Like the gift of discerning of spirits, the word of knowledge is also one of the nine gifts of the Spirit listed in 1 Corinthians 12:7–10, only this gift is different in its operation. It is the supernatural knowing of a fact, either present or past, and one you could not know unless the Holy Spirit showed it to you. This word of knowledge came as a sudden knowing on the inside of me. I asked him, "Do you watch horror movies?" He responded affirmatively. In this situation, he did not need to forgive someone for hurting him. What he needed was to repent for his sin of watching these terrible movies. I then led him in a prayer of repentance and cast the demon out of him.[4]

The Bible is clear about what we are to think and meditate on. We read this instruction:

> Finally, brethren, whatever things are true, whatever things are noble, whatever things are just, whatever things are pure, whatever things are lovely, whatever things are of good report, if there is any virtue and if there is anything praiseworthy—meditate on these things.
>
> Philippians 4:8

Simply put, you cannot entertain yourself with fear and not become demonized as a result.

When Sexual Shame Causes Fear

Malin was the third of four children and born into a household that neglected and abused her from birth. She grew up often not knowing when she would get her next meal and did not have her basic needs met. Her parents divorced, and she discovered only later that her mother had severe depression and schizophrenia. "My mother would lie on her bed in her room from morning until night and smoke cigarettes constantly," said Malin. "At night, she would rip me from my bed while sound asleep and take off with me in the car, believing she was being chased by someone." In one scenario after another, her mother subjected her to horrible situations with adult men. "I was sexually abused by my mother's boyfriends, friends, whoever they were, between the ages of six months and twelve years old," she said. "I woke up in unfamiliar beds with men I didn't know, and I don't remember how I got there."

To survive horrific abuse, Malin began to split and dissociate within her soul. When she was older, she turned to drugs, alcohol and sex just to cope with the intense emotional pain she always felt. "I felt a deep sense of shame and struggled to feel safe in general," Malin shared. "My identity was that of an abused, broken, smashed up and dirty child." Her mother moved her and her siblings to the other side of the country and surprisingly enrolled her in a Christian school. Her mother also told everyone she could, including her new school principal, what had happened to Malin, something that only perpetuated Malin's feelings of shame and fearful distrust. But her life changed after her school principal initiated a very compassionate and on-point discussion with her.

"My principal found me at school and sat down next to me to chat," Malin explained. "He told me about a man named Jesus who loves me and knows the reason for all of my tears." Malin reacted at first and began to shut down in pain the moment she heard Jesus was a "man." She did not want any relationship with any "man" as far as she was concerned.

Still, her principal pressed in and invited her to receive Jesus.

"It was the turning point of my life. Finally, I understood there was more to my life than being broken and abused." Malin became a born-again Christian at age fourteen. Her relationship with Jesus was real and genuine, but it did not take the pain or the memories away instantly. She needed to heal and to learn how to walk out of brokenness, deep shame and a reactionary fear that accompanied it. The good news is Malin is now a wife and mother of three and having the best time of her life, although she is still healing.

Can you relate to her story at all? Are you a Christian who loves Jesus, only you have a driving fear rooted in sexual shame to still contend with? Malin's story might seem extreme, but I have heard countless numbers of stories from outwardly successful men and women—all Christians—who were healing from sexual abuse or walking out of perverse lifestyles. And this shame caused them to live in unhealthy fear.

Healthy Fear vs. Unhealthy Fear

There is healthy fear and then there is unhealthy fear. For example, we need to have a healthy fear of the Lord. According to Joan Hunter in her book *Annihilate Fear*, the fear of the Lord is "reverence toward God, an attitude of awe and wonder at God's greatness and His marvelous ways. It means to honor, obey, respect, reverence, and worship Him."[5] She also contrasts true godly fear with the "hellfire and brimstone" messages preached by evangelists and pastors in times past. She wrote, "Scaring people into heaven is not from God."[6]

Healthy fear also keeps us safe and away from danger. Healthy fear will alert us that a high cliff is unsafe, that a shady person may be dangerous and not to swim too far from the ocean shore.[7] As parents, we train our children to have healthy fear for a variety of things just to keep them safe. We teach them to not touch a hot stove, not to ingest cleaning chemicals, to watch for cars when they cross a street and to not talk to strangers.

Fear becomes unhealthy fear when we are living life in response to danger that is not real. For example, Malin (see section above) was subjected to her mother's unhealthy fear, which was the belief that she was being chased by someone. It was not real. Her mother was being driven by an unhealthy, hallucinative kind of fear. The Bible says that this kind of fear comes from a demon. The apostle Paul gave these words to his protégé Timothy: "For God has not given us a spirit of fear, but of power and of love and of a sound mind" (2 Timothy 1:7).

If you are wondering at all if fear is just an overwhelming emotion or if it has spiritual dimensions, consider that there are over a hundred categorized phobias, ranging from claustrophobia, the fear of confined spaces, to nyctophobia, the fear of the dark. They have even categorized something called scoptophobia, which is the fear of being stared at.[8] They might be called phobias by the medical community, but all of these phobias are rooted in a spirit of fear. A spirit of fear can afflict an individual, but it can also afflict entire regions and even nations.

Mass Hysteria

In 1999, mass hysteria swept the nations over the Y2K (Year 2000) computer glitch that threatened to shut down the world's computers, power stations and building-control systems at the onset of the year 2000. When complex computer programs were first written in the 1960s, engineers used a two-digit code for the year, leaving out the "19." As the year 2000 approached, many believed that the systems would not interpret the "00" correctly, therefore causing a major failure in the global system.[9]

Personally, I recall how people went into a hoarding mentality in reaction to this perceived crisis. Collectively they emptied grocery store shelves, took money out of their bank accounts, bought generators and prepared for the worst. The Church, generally speaking, was divided on the issue. There were some pastors and congregants that refused to be alarmed while others were optimistic but cautious. Of course, there were the usual Christian media giants pushing an apocalyptic message along with their books and preparedness kits. There were also susceptible pastors who succumbed to the Y2K doomsday messages and pushed them strongly in their pulpits.[10]

Then midnight Y2K struck, and nothing happened at all. Airplanes did not fall out of the sky, cars and ground transportation continued uninterrupted, and bank accounts did not get wiped out as predicted. Some believed it was all a big hoax, but it was not. There was a problem, but programmers behind the scenes worked on the problem. Still, nefarious forces had propagated mass fear through the internet and news media while opportunistic Christians tipped the Church's emotional scales into an apocalyptic frenzy. How did Y2K mania take over so much of God's Church? Looking back, too many people turned to the internet for news and did not discern the plethora of false news and propaganda. They also did not know how to hear the voice of God through the noise of mass hysteria.

Thankfully, the Holy Spirit spoke to my husband and I the same message. He told us to not prepare for disaster, to not hoard any supplies or possessions, and that Y2K doomsday predictions would be like nothing. My husband spoke this to our church, and many listened. We still had a sample of congregants who had been mesmerized by the Christian media's apocalyptic messengers. In their fright, they still bought power generators and stockpiled food and guns up until the first day of the year 2000. Leaning into God's peace and promises in times like these would still need to be learned by God's Church in the years to come.

Less than a decade later, we experienced the American housing crash and then a subsequent recession. This was on the heels of what many believed to be predatory lending practices in which various lenders gave loans to homebuyers that they were unable to afford.[11] Mass defaults on home loans swept across the United States, which led to the stock market crash of 2008. When we drove through our neighborhood, for example, there were signs posted on house after house announcing foreclosures and bank sales. Many people had walked away from their new family homes and stopped paying their mortgages altogether.

Once again, crazy fear swept the nation, and people began hoarding their money. There was a widespread reactionary fear of serious financial meltdown. We discovered that many Christians did not know or trust God's promises for provision. They obeyed their fears and even withheld the Lord's tithes and offerings from their churches, with some churches shutting down as a result. My husband and I learned to trust God on an entirely new level during this season. We had always taught our church God's biblical instructions for giving tithes and offerings, and then how to sow financial seeds intentionally and reap His financial provision. When God is your Source, you will prosper in any situation. We were grateful to still finish a sizeable construction project that we had started just before the crash. Our only setback consisted of a few staff cutbacks—the first staff cutbacks since we had been there.

There was a choking fear that hung on to people for months as our nation navigated through this financial crisis. The Holy Spirit spoke His strategic remedy to the heart of my husband. He told him to start a feeding program for the poor in our city and reminded him that those who give to the poor will never lack (see Proverbs 28:27). Although the entire season was a walk of faith, one I will never forget, God did provide. The hardest part in battling mass fear was staying above its mental chokehold every day and keeping our faith fixed perfectly on Jehovah Jireh, the Lord our Provider. Eventually, this all passed, and financial confidence was restored back to the general public and also to God's Church.

It is another decade later, and once again the spirit of fear has shaken the nations with mass hysteria. I had just finished a powerful Inner Healing and Deliverance Institute with Katie Souza and Apostle John Eckhard at Harvest Church in Turlock, California. I then headed out to San Francisco with my Australian guest for sightseeing before her departure back home. I had no idea that the world was going to change in less than one week. At the hotel, the concierge let us know that some things were closing down in the city due to a potential pandemic. As we went out and about, it appeared the city was not taking the news too seriously. Everything was still mostly open with some modifications here and there. We finished our shopping and touring, and then I dropped my guest off at the airport. To our abrupt shock, she was quarantined to her home for two weeks upon her arrival back into Australia. And within just days, our entire life and ministry was put on hold.

News of pandemic, disease and death began to roll through the news media and the internet like a tsunami storm. Fourteen days of an initial mandatory shutdown turned into more than a year. I watched fear drive people into numerous hyperreactions, such as hoarding and boarding in their homes for months at a time. There were angry words and altercations breaking out in the public and throughout social media against those who either wore or did not wear a health mask depending on personal convictions. We experienced the usual division among Christians, although the political climate and presidential election fueled much of that in my opinion. I never contracted COVID but knew many who did. What I observed much more than people getting a virus was the debilitating fear that drove them into a kind of madness. When you are oppressed by a spirit of fear, you will not have a sound mind. It is a crazy-making spirit.

The spirit of fear does not just attack individuals but wants to shake and destroy entire nations. I am convinced that masses of people are in great need of traditional deliverance after the pandemic scare of 2020. Wherever fear is allowed to rule, it will steal God's blessings from you. We have to come out of agreement with the spirit of fear and every cluster of spirits that came upon the nations through the doorway of fear.

Fear Will Steal Your Blessings

In Egypt, the Israelites encountered outstanding miracles upon their exodus from slavery and bondage. In Exodus chapters 4–14, God demanded of Pharoah through Moses to "let My people go" and then signed His powerful decree with immediate acts of judgment. The Egyptians were then attacked with multiple plagues and pestilences and the entire land's water supply supernaturally turned to blood. A terrifying and felt darkness came and permeated the entire Egyptian nation, while the territory of the Israelites remained in natural sunlight. Finally, the death angel came and struck down every firstborn in Egypt but left the Israelite families and livestock untouched. The grand finale was the miraculous parting of the Red Sea. It parted as Moses raised his hand over the waters, and the Israelites passed through the sea on dry land all the while being pursued by the Egyptian armies. Once they passed through, Moses raised his hand again and the waters returned to their place and drowned their Egyptian pursuers. This was their unforgettable exodus from a terrible stronghold. Still, God never takes you out of something without bringing you into something.

God had promised the Israelites a good and large land, "a land flowing with milk and honey" (Exodus 3:8). When they arrived at the borders, the Israelites sent twelve spies to survey the land. The entire landscape dripped with abundance, only the fortified inhabitants needed to be displaced. After God's mighty release from Egyptian bondage, ten of the twelve spies still lost their nerve. They turned spineless on God and everyone else and gave the land some bad press. Their fearful reports served to unnerve the entire Israelite nation. God responded to their fear and unbelief by denying that generation their promise. They became permanent wanderers in the desert for forty years until they all died off.

"Fear is a prophet spirit from hell," said Jimmy Evans, author and co-host for *MarriageToday*, a syndicated television show. "It tells us lies about the future to get us to react in fear and not obey by faith."[12] The spirit of fear is a thief. It stops you from risking. It stops you from trusting God.

Fear is the opposite of faith. The way we defeat the spirit of fear is by having faith in God and in God's words. Joshua and Caleb were the two original spies who had faith in God and were preserved instead of dying off. Joshua also became Moses' successor and led the next-gen Israelites into their promise of the land. God commanded Joshua firmly to be courageous and to not be afraid. It was fear that stole the blessing of land from the previous generation. There was plenty of opportunity to be afraid, and if Joshua obeyed his fears, another generation would be forced to wander the desert once again. Sufficient faith, however, does not just appear on the inside of us. It is something we have to cultivate.

Cultivating Miracle-Receiving Faith

I had mentioned previously that God will release the Holy Spirit's gift of faith upon you to receive aspects of inner healing and deliverance. There are some things that will not heal or leave you without this gift in operation. If you are going to understand the gift of faith, however, you will first need to understand faith in general.

The first category of faith is *saving faith*. This is faith that leads us to salvation in Christ. The apostle Paul explained, "God saved you by his grace when you believed. And you can't take credit for this; it is a gift from God" (Ephesians 2:8 NLT). The second is *general faith*, which every believer has. We read, "As God has dealt to each one a measure of faith" (Romans 12:3). The third is the *fruit of faith*, or faithfulness, which is a fruit of the Holy Spirit in our lives. Those who have developed the fruit of faith will not quit their relationship with Jesus no matter what. And the last category is the *gift of faith*. The gift of faith is one of the nine gifts of the Holy Spirit mentioned in 1 Corinthians 12:7–10 ("to another faith by the same Spirit") and is supernatural faith and not ordinary faith. The gift of faith allows you to receive miracles.

God has dealt to each of us a measure of faith, but your faith has to be cultivated. Faith begins with God's Word, which is likened to a seed being planted inside of our hearts.[13] Faith is something that can grow, and it grows as we hear and rehearse God's promises for our lives continually.[14] We read in Hebrews 11 that faith is the substance of what we hope for and the evidence of things coming to us from God that we do not see happening just yet, and by faith we will obtain a good testimony.[15] Faith then knows God's Word and believes it is true, even if it has not transpired yet. Faith will also put you in position to receive God's promises actualized in your life. Finally, a lifestyle that cultivates faith will create conditions for the gift of faith to be activated. Miraculously, the gift of faith will heal the parts of you that have been shattered, fragmented and broken to pieces and are in need of a supernatural miracle to recover.

You Have Been Weaponized

Last year, I was in England conducting a prophetic conference. Traveling and ministering like this continued to be rewarding and fruitful, providing a healthy distraction. I was still having a myriad of recovered memories and felt I was losing my battle to "a living nightmare," as I had termed it. At the same time, there was a greater anointing for miracles upon my life, the kind of miracles I have never seen happen before. Whenever these ministry conferences ended, the anointing would lift as it did normally, and I would then sink back into an angry, emotional despair. In His goodness, God spoke to my heart powerfully while I was in London. He said, "Satan tried everything to defeat you. You didn't get defeated. You got weaponized." When I heard His words, a glimmer of faith came into my heart. It was just a glimmer, but Jesus compared Kingdom faith to a mustard seed in the gospels.[16] A mustard seed is about one or two millimeters in diameter but can grow twenty to thirty feet tall. In other words, your tiny mustard seed of faith can grow to great size and strength and command large mountains to move out of the way.

The prophetic conference in England had finished. I left the conference space to attend a few training meetings nearby at a Baptist church. I then preached their Sunday morning service and noticed a girl in her twenties who was seated in a wheelchair. She was slumped over her chair with her eyes closed and head resting upon her hand. She was physically weak and fatigued, but she had not been in the wheelchair for that long. Whatever she was dealing with was something recent. As I looked more closely, I noticed a few familiar things. I noticed how she looked very much like I did after my body collapsed during my junior year of high school. Right then, I knew what her problem was. I knew she had been raped and her body had buckled under the force of the trauma. I then asked if I could pray for her privately once the service ended.

I finished ministering and closed the service. I was then led to a back room and found her waiting for me. The young woman told me her story, a story that confirmed what I had already thought had happened. She described how she had been date-raped and now had debilitating fatigue and other complications. She could hardly walk, and her entire life had been put on hold.

With that, I shared that I, too, had been drugged and raped in high school and had a similar physical reaction. "I didn't know Jesus during that time in my life, but you do," I explained. "What I did know was how to take my body back." I further explained that rape is the equivalent of having your body stolen from you, and it will not be politely returned. "You have to take back everything that was stolen from you, including your body," I emphasized. "I've been sent here by God to show you that it can be done."

Something about my words impacted her. She looked at me, and faith rose up inside of her. When faith rose up in her, she rose up out of her wheelchair. She then walked out of the room and into the sanctuary, leaving her wheelchair behind. Everyone who remained in the sanctuary stared in wonder as she walked out of the building like a totally new person.

This miracle happened with my mustard seed of faith. If God moved this powerfully when I was this sick on the inside, what will He do when I am well? This is why I am telling my story. I am still healing, but I know how to heal. I know how to find a word from God for any situation that comes my way. I know how to believe and press in for that word until it comes to pass. That is my secret, and it works every single time. I also know this book has stirred up your faith. Now you know that you are not too far gone, and you can recover from the worst of the worst. Someday, you will tell your story, too.

MY **PRAYER** FOR YOU

Holy Spirit, I ask You to bring freedom to the hearts and minds of readers who have lived in bondage to a spirit of fear. Seal the healing words of this book to their hearts and finish the good work You have begun in each of them. Give them the heart of a finisher as they continue their inner healing and deliverance journey unto completeness. I make the decree: They will overcome it all and tell their stories to the masses. In Jesus' name, Amen.

KINGDOM REFLECTIONS

1. Some demonic manifestations are caused by the spirit of fear (see 2 Timothy 1:7). There are different reasons, or root causes, that open a door for this spirit to oppress someone.

2. The spirit of fear can afflict an individual, but it can also afflict entire regions and even nations with mass hysteria.

3. Fear will steal your blessings. You have to come out of agreement with it and obey God's Word by faith.

4. Faith is something we cultivate and grow as we rehearse God's promises for our lives. By faith, we will have a good testimony.

5. There is also the Holy Spirit's gift of faith, which is supernatural faith and not ordinary faith. Aspects of inner healing and deliverance will need supernatural faith to recover.

KINGDOM QUESTIONS

1. Have you ever considered the spiritual dimensions of fear, that it is a spirit more than a negative emotion?

2. There is healthy fear and unhealthy fear. Unhealthy fear is living life in response to danger that is not real. Is this something you struggle with?

3. After reading this chapter and the section about mass hysteria, what are your reflections?

4. Were you able to say the prayer of deliverance from fear (located in appendix B) out loud? Did you notice anything shift inside of you as a result?

5. Do you understand the difference between general faith and the gift of faith? How do they promote inner healing and deliverance?

Appendix A

Healing from Satanic Ritual Abuse

"Therefore whoever hears these sayings of Mine, and does them, I will liken him to a wise man who built his house on the rock: and the rain descended, the floods came, and the winds blew and beat on that house; and it did not fall, for it was founded on the rock."

Matthew 7:24–25

People have asked me if they can heal from SRA using traditional self-deliverance models. Self-deliverance involves praying through the bindings and curses by yourself and then seeking emotional healing with God by yourself. I wish it was that easy, but usually it is not. Understanding the basics of self-deliverance will help you in the lighter matters, but you will need help from skilled ministers and therapists for multiple incidents and deep-level SRA. You will not overcome this fully by yourself, and it will become your stuck place.

Still, you will want to listen carefully to the Holy Spirit as He helps you to heal, close doors and put things in order as He intends for them to be. For example, my husband and I felt the Holy Spirit's leading to renew our wedding vows after it came to light that I had been forcibly married as a young teenager in a pagan ceremony. What a beautiful finale to something so horrible.

For SRA survivors, you can never predict when recovered memories will surface. When it happens, it is comparable to being emotionally punched in the gut or the jaw. You have to stop what you are doing and just let it come up, even if it comes up ugly. Next, you have to assess the damage and make a plan to heal. This is what life is like for those who have lived through SRA. You go from shock to shock, and it can seem as if it will never end. If you are emotionally equipped enough, you will know how to stay functional and move through it constructively even though you will not avoid it. You have to look at every instance of memory recovery as an opportunity to heal. The memory has come up for a reason.

This has been my life every day since my memories began to return. I am very functional and have gained the skills to work through the most horrible recollections, but I know many who are not yet able to do that. If this is you, I am praying for you to get grounded and solid in your faith in Jesus Christ. What happened to you was diabolical, but Jesus will redeem you and restore you with an exclamation point. He will teach you how to build your house, meaning your entire self, on the rock of His words so you do not sink and lose your battle.

Do you know people who are experiencing trauma from SRA? If so, here are some things you can do to help them:

1. *Listen to their stories.* Every time they speak their truth, it becomes more real to them. They might have to say it several times to you. It has to become real to them so they can move through the details and make a plan to overcome it. Their stories will be horrific. Use reflective listening and validate what they are saying. Saying things like, "I believe you" and "You are going to make it" will go a long way.

2. *Do not try to fix it.* They will not know if they are going to make it through for a long time. Just listen and offer prayer that lifts and comforts them. Really learn how to sit with the hurting. Also, believe that Jesus does heal the worst of the worst because your faith will be challenged when you hear what they went through. I assure you from personal experience, they are not too far gone.

3. *Encourage them to get proper help.* They must have professional Christian counseling with someone who understands and has experience with complex trauma. Still, it is a rare find for a therapist to understand the spiritual dynamics of SRA. They will need inner healing and deliverance ministry, too.

If you have survived SRA, I want you to know you are ready for this. Now you can do the work to get that part of your heart back, and you want to regain as much of the lost parts of your heart that you can. Remember the proverb, "Keep your heart with all diligence, for out of it spring the issues of life" (Proverbs 4:23). Healing will bring new life to you, and it will be noticeable and measurable. You *can* recover all.

Prayers for Inner Healing and Deliverance

"I will not drive them out from before you in one year, lest the land become desolate and the beasts of the field become too numerous for you. Little by little I will drive them out from before you, until you have increased, and you inherit the land."

Exodus 23:29–30

A significant part of personal freedom is knowing how to pray in alignment with God's Word over yourself. God created everything with a word, and you and I will do likewise, because "death and life are in the power of the tongue, and those who love it will eat its fruit" (Proverbs 18:21). Be confident knowing that you can use your own voice to initiate healing and deliverance in your life, as well as in ministry to others.

Prayers to Pray over Yourself

The following prayers are designed to help you begin to pray effectively. These prayers will help you to articulate needed points of repentance and deliverance while inviting the work of the Holy Spirit within your life and heart. Keep in mind that some people can experience change rather quickly, but more often healing happens progressively, as you have to grow into your personal freedom in order to keep it.

A Prayer for Freedom from Hatred

If you are bound to hatred personally or generationally, I want to invite you to pray this prayer out loud:

Heavenly Father, I come to You in the name of Jesus and confess that I have held hatred in my heart. I forgive (name of person or persons) for harming me. I repent for using hatred for power and protection instead of going to You for counsel, protection and help. I ask You to come and heal the wound in my heart that they caused with their words and actions. I also command any demonic harasser, tormentor or oppressor to leave me now in the name of Jesus. I repent now for the sins of my ancestors who hated each other, who hated other nationalities and who hated people in general. I command the spirit of hatred and murder to leave my bloodline and to leave my children and every generation after me in Jesus' name. Holy Spirit, I invite You to saturate me now with Your tangible presence. Amen.

A Prayer of Repentance and Renunciation from the Occult

This simple prayer will get you started, but due to the nature of the occult, you will have to be as specific as you can.

In the name of Jesus, I repent of any and all occult rituals made by me or my forefathers. I renounce all dedications made by me or my forefathers to cults, cult leaders and their demons. I break all ungodly and binding covenants associated with cults and occult practices both to demons and human beings. I break every claim for my life or my family through demonic rituals, dedications and ungodly covenants. I dedicate myself and my family fully to the Lordship of Jesus Christ. Holy Spirit, I now invite You to come and be the ruling Spirit over my life and my family in Jesus' name.

As you say this prayer of repentance and renunciation, list to the best of your ability the specific practices, the specific cults, the names of demons, deities and people that you bound yourself to or your family bound themselves to. You might consider doing this with a mature Christian friend or Christian prayer counselor in case there is a manifestation that occurs with you personally or in your physical surroundings. For example, those breaking free from satanism have experienced objects supernaturally moving around their home or in their environment in manifestation. Others, such as myself, have experienced demons not wanting to release their claim and the spiritual warfare associated with that. If this happens, you need to commit yourself to working it through, all the way through, until freedom manifests, because it belongs to you in His name.

List of common occult practices:

- Astrology
- Chakra reading
- Channeling
- Charmary
- Clairvoyance
- Coffee grounds reading
- Divination
- Enchantments
- Extr-Sensory Perception (ESP)
- Fortune-telling
- Grave soaking
- Hexes
- Horoscopes
- Idol worship
- Incantations and spells
- Magic (all forms)
- Mediums
- Nature worship
- Necromancy
- Omens
- Ouija boards
- Palm reading
- Parapsychology
- Psychic readings
- Psychokinesis
- Reiki
- Sacrifices (all forms)
- Seances
- Sending energy
- Sorcery
- Spirit guides
- Taglocking
- Tarot cards
- Tea leaves reading
- Telepathy
- Transcendental meditation
- Witchcraft
- Wizardry
- Yoga

Again, there are always nuances within the various cult and occultic frameworks that will need to be evaluated, repented of and renounced. For example, Freemasonry engages a plethora of rituals and curses that will need to be addressed through deliverance prayer. Again, this removes the legal claims that demons will attempt to use against you and your family to wreak havoc spiritually, physically, mentally, financially, etc. You can easily find many suggested prayer guides for this specifically on the internet by typing in "prayers to break Freemasonry." A resource to break free from Freemasonry is located here: https://jubileeresources .org/pages/freemasonry.

A Prayer of Repentance for the Jezebel Spirit

Make this prayer your own:

Heavenly Father, I recognize and acknowledge before You the areas of my life that reflect the spirit and attributes of Jezebel. I repent of manipulation, control, insubordination, false repentance, sexual immorality, rage, intimidation and pride. I put these attributes to death at the cross of Your Son, Jesus Christ, and with Your help will no longer use these demonic tools to live my life. I forgive my abusers and release them fully to You. I surrender my life and ask You to change me from the inside out. Lead me in the way I should go and direct my heart toward righteousness in the Holy Spirit.

A Prayer of Deliverance from Shame

Here are some timeless promises written as declarations to help you rise out of shame. Consider these promises to be a healing balm to your heart and soul. Also consider them to be effective weapons of warfare when thoughts of shame show up justified in your mind.

Say this out loud:

- *God has rolled away all of my reproach* (see Joshua 5:9).
- *I have put my trust in the Lord. I will not be put to shame* (see Psalm 71:1).
- *I will not fear. I will not be ashamed nor disgraced. I will not be put to shame and will forget the shame of my youth. I will not remember the reproach of widowhood anymore* (see Isaiah 54:4).
- *Instead of my shame I will have double honor. Instead of confusion, I will rejoice in my portion. In my land I will possess double and have everlasting joy* (see Isaiah 61:7).
- *I belong to God and I believe God. I will never be put to shame* (see Joel 2:26–27; Romans 9:33; 10:11; 1 Peter 2:6).
- *I walk according to the Spirit and not the flesh. I am not condemned* (see Romans 8:1).
- *I have been adopted by God, showered in His love, and I am accepted and loved as much as Jesus is loved by God our Father* (see Ephesians 1:5–6).
- *Because of Jesus, I am completely shameless.*
- *I speak to shame now and command SHAME OFF ME.*

A Prayer of Deliverance from Fear

Say this out loud:

In Jesus' name, I repent and renounce every spirit of fear and every spirit that has afflicted me through the doorway of fear. I command fear of sickness, plague, disease, infirmity and COVID to go. The fear of dying and premature death and destruction must leave me now. I refuse the fear of lack, poverty, joblessness, not succeeding, not prospering, not having enough, lost business and lost income. The fear of the unknown and having an uncertain future, I repent of it and fear not! I repent and renounce spirits of depression, weariness, sadness, isolation, loneliness, hopelessness, despondency, despair and discouragement. I repent and renounce spirits of anger, frustration, rage, violence and abuse. I refuse all spirits of grief, hurt and despair over lost loved ones. I repent and renounce all spirits of alcohol, drug addiction and any addiction in Jesus' name. I command spirits of stress, worry, anxiety, confusion in the mind, mental breakdown, insanity, nervousness, panic attacks to go. I have a sound mind! I command every spirit of hell released through bad news and bad news reports to leave and never return. I command spirits of unbelief, doubt, backsliding and lost intimacy with God to go. In Jesus' name, I bind and forbid the strongman and the ruling spirit of this nation from afflicting me with fear in any way. Thank You, Jesus, for abundant life, long life, Psalm 91 life, and for delivering me from every fear assignment from hell. Thank You for Your joy, peace, health, favor and abundant prosperity.

MY FINAL **PRAYER** FOR YOU

I am believing for the gift of working of miracles to be released as I pray a prayer of reknitting over you:

Heavenly Father, You knew them before they were born and You spoke a good word over their lives. You knit them in their mother's womb, fashioned them and prepared them with everything they need for this life. Even now in this season of recovering, they have what they need. Holy Spirit, I ask You to come and reknit them where they have been torn to pieces. Come and heal the tears, the fragments, their deep brokenness. Reknit and renew them in their spirits and in the spirit of their minds. I ask You to work miraculously in the day and while they sleep and dream at night. Make them a living testimony of Your goodness, in the name of Jesus. Amen.

In Remembrance

When my buried childhood memories began to resurface at age forty-seven, only to reveal the most horrific details of my life, I promised myself and God to find a way to still honor one person I could not forget. For those with traumatic or dissociative amnesia,[1] even significant memories can remain deeply buried in your psyche—that is, until you are ready to remember them. This was one of those memories, although there have been many more. With that said, I wrote this book in final dedication and remembrance of my deceased friend Enrique.

Enrique and I held a secret friendship while entrapped inside an occult child trafficking network based in Hollywood. I am unsure at what age Enrique and I first met or how he became involved in this next part, but he had been given charge to keep me and others like me organized within a housing structure for access by patrons of this network. As I described earlier, the housing structure was an actual mansion somewhere in Southern California, and I was there for a very short period of time. Also, I do not know how I came into that establishment or how I got out. My memories are completely blank on that information. Patrons of this establishment sought to engage in the full spectrum of ritual and sexual abuse of minors, making the environment horribly violent and punitive. Because of our relationship, Enrique would defer, overlook and deny requests that would have subjected me to the worst elements of this network seeking what this mansion had to offer. He was caught protecting me and was executed as punishment.

My memories are still very incomplete, but I believe I was the last person to see him alive before he was murdered. His killers sought to erase his young life from existence along with the plethora of sinister secrets that he carried. Instead, those evil agents buried him like a seed into the dark earth only to have him spring forth decades later within my newly awakened memories.

When my memory of him resurfaced, I began to mourn his death and grieve the terrible loss of my friend as if it had just happened. Again, this is a normal response when buried memories are recovered, even if decades after the fact. At the same time, something about his memory began to pull me back together. I had been torn apart on the inside for close to three years, simply unable to accept the devastating facts of my life that had come raging to the surface. I fought hard in my mind to believe any of this was real.

As I was beginning to really grieve Enrique's death, Jesus spoke to me late one evening with perfect clarity. He said, *I understand what you are feeling. My friend was executed, too.* I believe He was referring to John the Baptist, and I could have never created that response on my own. That simple conversation with Jesus both comforted my heart and finally made everything real. I accepted the truth of my life and quit believing I was making everything up and losing my mind. At the same time, a faith from the Holy Spirit entered into me. I knew without a doubt I would see total recovery despite all odds.

Enrique was denied a proper funeral and family to mourn his death. His epitaph was neither written nor even considered—that is, until now. Almost fully forgotten, his memory can now live on through the writing and publishing of this book. It was this recovered memory of his life and death that prompted my decision to write about my journey more openly. Justice does not always come instantly, but it does come eventually and often in unusual ways. My prayer is that this book brings not only justice to Enrique, but also justice to the countless other victims who have suffered like him, and like us, and were never given a voice to speak out.

Until now.

Notes

Chapter 1 Do You Want to Be Made Whole?

1. Revelation 12:7–9:
   And war broke out in heaven: Michael and his angels fought with the dragon; and the dragon and his angels fought, but they did not prevail, nor was a place found for them in heaven any longer. So the great dragon was cast out, that serpent of old, called the Devil and Satan, who deceives the whole world; he was cast to the earth, and his angels were cast out with him.

2. "And now, whereas my father put a heavy yoke on you, I will add to your yoke; my father chastised you with whips, but I will chastise you with scourges!" (1 Kings 12:11).

3. "Nazarite," *Easton's Bible Dictionary*, Bible Study Tools, https://www.biblestudytools.com/dictionary/nazarite/:
   Nazarite (Heb. form Nazirite), the name of such Israelites as took on them the vow prescribed in Numbers 6:2–21. The word denotes generally one who is separated from others and consecrated to God. Although there is no mention of any Nazarite before Samson, yet it is evident that they existed before the time of Moses. The vow of a Nazarite involved these three things, (1) abstinence from wine and strong drink, (2) refraining from cutting the hair off the head during the whole period of the continuance of the vow, and (3) the avoidance of contact with the dead. When the period of the continuance of the vow came to an end, the Nazarite had to present himself at the door of the sanctuary with (1) a he lamb of the first year for a burnt-offering, (2) a ewe lamb of the first year

for a sin-offering, and (3) a ram for a peace-offering. After these sacrifices were offered by the priest, the Nazarite cut off his hair at the door and threw it into the fire under the peace-offering.

4. "Immediately the Spirit drove Him into the wilderness. And He was there in the wilderness forty days, tempted by Satan, and was with the wild beasts; and the angels ministered to Him" (Mark 1:12–13).

5. Agape Bible Fellowship, "Mass Deliverance," Sermon Archive, https://www.agapebible.net/sermon-series/mass-deliverance/.

6. Dr. Ana Mendez Ferrell, *Regions of Captivity* (Ponte Vedra, Fla.: Voice of the Light Ministries, 2016), Kindle edition, 23.

7. Jesus always lives to make intercession for us, something often carried out through His Church on the earth. We do not always know how or what to pray, but when we partner with the Holy Spirit in prayer, we will pray the right prayer every time (see Hebrews 7:25; Romans 8:26).

8. Mark 16:15–18:

> And He said to them, "Go into all the world and preach the gospel to every creature. He who believes and is baptized will be saved; but he who does not believe will be condemned. And these signs will follow those who believe: In My name they will cast out demons; they will speak with new tongues; they will take up serpents; and if they drink anything deadly, it will by no means hurt them; they will lay hands on the sick, and they will recover."

9. "Is There Biblical Support for Parachurch Ministries?," Got Questions, https://www.gotquestions.org/parachurch-ministries.html:

> The definition of a Christian parachurch ministry is "a Christian faith-based organization which carries out its mission usually independent of church oversight." The prefix *para-* is Greek for "beside" or "alongside." Therefore, the parachurch ministry is one that seeks to come alongside the local church, providing in many cases that which the church is less able to provide on its own.

10. https://www.restoringthefoundations.org.

11. https://elijahhouse.org.

12. http://www.heartsyncministries.org.

13. http://bethelsozo.com.

14. Betty Tapscott, *Inner Healing through Healing of Memories* (Kingwood, Tex.: Hunter Publishing, 1987), 13.

15. John Eckhardt, *The Deliverance and Spiritual Warfare Manual* (Lake Mary, Fla., Charisma House, 2014), Kindle edition, chapter 2.

16. See Acts 10:38.

17. There are many examples of those who have brought deliverance on a regional level and beyond, but notable historymakers are Friar Danial Nash and Abel Cary, who interceded powerfully for the revival meetings

held by Charles Finney in New York State. Dr. Michael H. Yeagar, *Daniel Nash, A Man Mighty in Prayer: The Key to Revival* (2019).

18. "To console those who mourn in Zion, to give them beauty for ashes, the oil of joy for mourning, the garment of praise for the spirit of heaviness; that they may be called trees of righteousness, the planting of the LORD, that He may be glorified" (Isaiah 61:3).

Chapter 2 Dead Hearts Really Do Come Back to Life

1. When you become baptized in the Holy Spirit, you will speak in a brand-new language; only it is a heavenly language, not a natural one. Other terms for the same experience include *praying in the Spirit, speaking in an unknown tongue* and *receiving the promise of the Father*. To know more about receiving your spiritual language through Holy Spirit baptism, read the appendix of my book *Glory Carriers* (Minneapolis: Chosen, 2019).

2. "Then the LORD said to Satan, 'Have you considered My servant Job, that there is none like him on the earth, a blameless and upright man, one who fears God and shuns evil?'" (Job 1:8). Job came under a fierce spiritual battle with Satan, but God already knew Job's heart and said it. He knew that Job would remain loyal to Him.

3. *Tiananmen* means "the gate of heavenly peace." Wikipedia contributors, "Tiananmen," *Wikipedia, The Free Encyclopedia*, https://en.wikipedia.org/wiki/Tiananmen.

4. *Tianfu* means "gate of heavenly government," as translated by our Chinese host during an intercessory prayer trip in that nation.

5. This kind of intercession is something that should not be done by those who are new to prayer. If you do not know what you are doing, you can cause serious harm to yourself and your immediate family. To become equipped for higher-level intercession, read my book *The Intercessors Handbook* (Minneapolis: Chosen, 2016) and Cindy Jacobs, *Possessing the Gates of the Enemy*, rev. ed. (Minneapolis: Chosen, 2018).

6. Eivaz, *Glory Carriers*, 81–86.

7. The Bible refers to Leviathan in Psalms, Isaiah and the book of Job. A lengthy description is found in Job 41, beginning with verse 1: "Can you draw out Leviathan with a hook, or snare his tongue with a line which you lower?" It ends with, "He beholds every high thing; he is king over all the children of pride" (verse 34).

8. "It happened that as we were going to the place of prayer, a slave woman [possessed with] a spirit of divination met us, who was bringing great profit to her masters by fortune-telling" (Acts 16:16 NASB). The spirit of divination referred to in this verse is actually a python spirit and

historically believed to be the guardian spirit for the oracle of Delphi. Think of how a python spirit behaves in the natural, and you will get the picture. See Eivaz, *Glory Carriers*, 81–82.

9. Jennifer Eivaz, "God Is Bringing: Vindication, Restoration and Recompense!," The Elijah List, August 24, 2017, https://www.elijahlist.com /words/display_word.html?ID=18630.

10. In its simplest form, a prophecy is communication from God, either directly to a person or to a person through another person. It is one of the nine gifts of the Holy Spirit listed in 1 Corinthians 12:7–10. God will communicate His prophetic word in a variety of ways (see Hebrews 1:1). Prophetic words often need to be prayed over and brought before the Lord again and again over a period of time before they come to pass. To learn more, read my book *Prophetic Secrets* (Minneapolis: Chosen, 2020).

11. See also Jennifer Eivaz, "Prophetic Word for 2019: It's the Year of the Big Door," January 7, 2019, https://www.jennifereivaz.com/2019/01 /07/prophetic-word-for-2019-its-the-year-of-the-big-door/.

12. See Isaiah 61:7; Exodus 22:4, 7; 2 Kings 2:9.

13. Eivaz, "God Is Bringing."

Chapter 3 Hearts of Stone

1. "Science of the Heart: Exploring the Role of the Heart in Human Performance," HeartMath Institute, https://www.heartmath.org/research /science-of-the-heart/heart-brain-communication/; "The Brain-Gut Connection," Johns Hopkins Medicine, https://www.hopkinsmedicine .org/health/wellness-and-prevention/the-brain-gut-connection.

2. "G2588 – kardia," *Vine's Expository Dictionary of New Testament Words*, Blue Letter Bible, https://www.blueletterbible.org/search/dictionary /viewtopic.cfm?topic=VT0001335.

3. "Heart," *Easton's Bible Dictionary*, Blue Letter Bible, https://www .blueletterbible.org/search/dictionary/viewtopic.cfm?topic=ET0001699.

4. "What Is the Difference between Iniquity, Sin, and Transgression?," Got Questions, https://www.gotquestions.org/iniquity-sin-transgression .html.

5. "You shall not bow down to them nor serve them. For I, the LORD your God, am a jealous God, visiting the iniquity of the fathers upon the children to the third and fourth generations of those who hate Me" (Deuteronomy 5:9). Other references are Exodus 20:5; Exodus 34:7; Numbers 14:18.

6. "Does the Bible Mention David's Mother?," Got Questions, https:// www.gotquestions.org/David-mother.html:

Nahash was an Ammonite king (1 Samuel 11:1). Speculation suggests that David's mother had been married to Nahash when she bore the half sisters and then later became the second wife of Jesse. Further speculation implies that David's mother was not yet married to Jesse when she became pregnant—that perhaps she was still married to Nahash when she conceived David.

7. "David's Cry for Purity," *MacLaren's Expositions*, Bible Hub, https://biblehub.com/commentaries/psalms/51-10.htm; "Psalm 51:10," *Cambridge Bible for Schools and Colleges*, Bible Hub, https://biblehub.com/commentaries/psalms/51-10.htm.

8. "1254. bara'," *Brown-Driver-Briggs*, Bible Hub, https://biblehub.com/hebrew/1254.htm.

9. "Now when they heard this, they were cut to the heart" (Acts 2:37).

10. Psalm 27:10; 1 Samuel 17:28–29.

11. "Therefore it is of faith that it might be according to grace, so that the promise might be sure to all the seed, not only to those who are of the law, but also to those who are of the faith of Abraham, who is the father of us all" (Romans 4:16).

12. "It happened in the spring of the year, at the time when kings go out to battle, that David sent Joab and his servants with him, and all Israel; and they destroyed the people of Ammon and besieged Rabbah. But David remained at Jerusalem" (2 Samuel 11:1).

13. "And Jesus, walking by the Sea of Galilee, saw two brothers, Simon called Peter, and Andrew his brother, casting a net into the sea; for they were fishermen. Then He said to them, 'Follow Me, and I will make you fishers of men'" (Matthew 4:18–19).

14. Margot Rittenhouse, MS, LPC, NCC, "What Is Bulimia: Symptoms, Complications and Causes," Eating Disorder Hope, June 30, 2020, https://www.eatingdisorderhope.com/information/bulimia.

15. Jennifer Chesak, "Understanding Why People Cut Themselves, Hide It, and How to Help," Healthline, October 17, 2017, https://www.healthline.com/health/mental-health/why-do-people-cut-themselves #support.

16. "Repentance," Baker's Evangelical Dictionary of Biblical Theology, Bible Study Tools, https://www.biblestudytools.com/dictionary/repentance/:

> The most common term in the Old Testament for repentance is *sub*; the verbal forms appear well over 1,050 times, although translated "repent" only 13 times, and the substantive "repentance" occurs only once in the New International Version. More commonly the translation is "turn" or "return." . . . In the New Testament, the key term for repentance is metanoia [metavnoia]. It has two usual senses: a "change of mind" and "regret/remorse."

17. Vawter and Hoppe, quoted in David Guzik, "A New Covenant for Israel's Land and People," *Study Guide for Ezekiel 36*, Blue Letter Bible, https://www.blueletterbible.org/Comm/guzik_david/StudyGuide2017 -Eze/Eze-36.cfm.

18. Poole, quoted in Guzik, "A New Covenant for Israel's Land and People."

19. "The eyes of your understanding [hearts] being enlightened; that you may know what is the hope of His calling, what are the riches of the glory of His inheritance in the saints" (Ephesians 1:18). BibleGateway leaves a footnote for the word *understanding* to be translated "hearts" (https://www.biblegateway.com/passage/?search=Ephesians+1%3A18 &version=NKJV).

20. "But solid food is for the mature, who because of practice have their senses trained to distinguish between good and evil" (Hebrews 5:14 NASB).

21. "How the Brain Hides Memories," Northwestern Medicine, https://www.nm.org/healthbeat/medical-advances/how-the-brain-hides -traumatic-memories; Lisa Nosal, MFT, "Why Are Memories of My Past Trauma Coming Back Now?," Good Therapy, May 18, 2015, https://www .goodtherapy.org/blog/why-are-memories-of-my-past-trauma-coming -back-now-0518155.

Chapter 4 When You Hate Someone

1. "Hate (*n.*)," *The Merriam-Webster.com Dictionary*, https://www .merriam-webster.com/dictionary/hate.

2. Tanya Harell, "An Overview of Rage and What to Do about It," Better Help, May 21, 2020, https://www.betterhelp.com/advice/anger/an -overview-of-rage-what-to-do-about-it/.

3. Paraclete," *Baker's Evangelical Dictionary of Biblical Theology*, Bible Study Tools, https://www.biblestudytools.com/dictionary/paraclete /; "3875. paraklétos," *Strong's Concordance*, Bible Hub, https://biblehub .com/greek/3875.htm.

4. Kurt Selles, "The Holy Spirit as Counselor," *Today*, June 15, 2016, https://today.reframemedia.com/devotions/the-holy-spirit-as-counselor.

5. "Separatist," *The Encyclopedia Britannica*, https://www.britannica .com/topic/Separatists.

6. Wikipedia contributors, "William Brewster (Mayflower Passenger)," *Wikipedia, The Free Encyclopedia*, https://en.wikipedia.org/wiki/William _Brewster_(Mayflower_passenger).

7. Eivaz, *Prophetic Secrets*, chapter 2, referring to "What Does the Bible Say About Muslims/Islam?," Bibleinfo, https://www.bibleinfo.com /en/questions/what-does-bible-say-about-muslims-islam; "Is the Arab

Nation Descended from Ishmael?," CBN, https://www1.cbn.com/online discipleship/is-the-arab-nation-descended-from-ishmael%3F.

8. "You are of your father the devil, and the desires of your father you want to do. He was a murderer from the beginning, and does not stand in the truth, because there is no truth in him. When he speaks a lie, he speaks from his own resources, for he is a liar and the father of it" (John 8:44).

9. Alice Clark, "The Beginners Guide to Inner Healing," Transformation, School of Ministry, Catch the Fire, https://catchthefire.com/blog-full /the-beginners-guide-to-inner-healing.

10. "The Spirit of the LORD is upon Me, because He has anointed Me to preach the gospel to the poor; He has sent Me to heal the broken-hearted, to proclaim liberty to the captives and recovery of sight to the blind, to set at liberty those who are oppressed" (Luke 4:18).

Chapter 5 Traumatized and Shattered

1. "Writ," Cornell Law School, Legal Information Institute, https:// www.law.cornell.edu/wex/writ.

2. Robert Henderson, *Accessing the Courts of Heaven: Positioning Yourself for Breakthrough and Answered Prayers* (Shippensburg, Penn.: Destiny Image, 2017), n.p.

3. "Dissociative symptoms include the experience of detachment or feeling, as if one is outside one's body and a loss of memory or amnesia. Dissociative disorders are frequently associated with previous experience of trauma." There are different levels of dissociation, but children especially will mentally escape horrific scenes of abuse in their minds through dissociation that would have otherwise caused them to go insane. They will continue this pattern whenever triggered into adulthood until their minds are healed. "What Are Dissociative Disorders?" American Psychiatric Association, August 2018, https:// www.psychiatry.org/patients-families/dissociative-disorders/what-are -dissociative-disorders.

4. "He restores my soul" (Psalm 23:3). "And do not be conformed to this world, but be transformed by the renewing of your mind" (Romans 12:2). "You will find rest for your souls" (Matthew 11:29).

5. "What Is Trauma?," Integrated Listening Systems, https://inte gratedlistening.com/what-is-trauma/; "Trauma Definition," SAMHSA, https://web.archive.org/web/20140805161505/http://www.samhsa.gov /traumajustice/traumadefinition/definition.aspx.

6. "PSTD vs. Trauma," Hope and Healing Center & Institute, https:// hopeandhealingcenter.org/ptsd-vs-trauma/.

7. "What Is the Difference between PTSD and Complex PTSD?," Greenwood Counseling Center, https://greenwoodcounselingcenter.com/difference-ptsd-complex-ptsd/.

8. Ibid.

9. Ibid.

10. Wikipedia contributors, "Marilyn Van Derbur," *Wikipedia, The Free Encyclopedia*, https://en.wikipedia.org/wiki/Marilyn_Van_Derbur.

11. "Marilyn Van Derbur—You Have to Confront the Terror," Darkness to Light, March 12, 2010, https://www.d2l.org/marilyn-van-derbur-you-have-to-confront-the-terror/.

12. Ibid.

13. Rick Renner, "Healing the Brokenhearted," https://renner.org/devotionals/healing-the-brokenhearted.

14. Ibid.

15. "Do not be deceived, God is not mocked; for whatever a man sows, that he will also reap" (Galatians 6:7). Although this verse is addressing negative and sinful sowing and the consequences, there is an opposite truth that we can sow to the things of God and reap His blessings and benefits instead.

16. Diane Langburg, "Complex Trauma: Understanding and Treatment," YouTube video, January 21, 2016, https://www.youtube.com/watch?v=otxAuHG9hKo&t=1230s, 21:33, 40:00, 41:54.

17. "Therefore choose life, that both you and your descendants may live" (Deuteronomy 30:19).

18. David J. Ley, Ph.D., "Forget Me Not: The Persistent Myth of Repressed Memories," *Psychology Today*, October 6, 2019. https://www.psychologytoday.com/us/blog/women-who-stray/201910/forget-me-not-the-persistent-myth-of-repressed-memories. Author's note: When I researched the credentials of this published psychologist, this would not be someone with a clear Christian frame of reference. This might be what undergirds his belief that repressed memories in association with SRA is a myth. The debate over repressed memories emerged in the 1990s and is still the subject of controversy, however. "Scientists and Practitioners Don't See Eye to Eye on Repressed Memory," Association for Psychological Science, Dec. 13, 2013. https://www.psychologicalscience.org/news/releases/scientists-and-practitioners-dont-see-eye-to-eye-on-repressed-memory.html.

19. Tweet @DianeLangberg, https://twitter.com/DianeLangberg/status/1387436562791735302.

20. Tweet, @DianeLangberg, https://twitter.com/DianeLangberg/status/1382302612805054470.

21. This story has been adapted from the book by Heather Davediuk Gringich, *Restoring the Shattered Self. A Christian Counselor's Guide to Complex Trauma* (Downers Grove, Illinois, IVP Academic, n.d.), Kindle edition, 13.

Chapter 6 Deliverance from Cults and Occult Practices

1. "Santeria (*n.*)," *The Merriam-Webster.com Dictionary*, www.merriam-webster.com/dictionary/Santeria.

2. S. A. Tower, *From the Craft to Christ* (USA: Dwell Publishing, 2019), Kindle version, chapter 12.

3. Wikipedia contributors, "Occult," *Wikipedia, The Free Encyclopedia*, https://en.wikipedia.org/wiki/occult; "Cult or Occult?" English Plus, http://englishplus.com/grammar/00000205.htm.

4. Ibid.

5. "What Does It Mean to Be a Born-Again Christian?" Got Questions, https://www.gotquestions.org/born-again.html.

6. Ibid.

7. The Church of Jesus Christ of Latter Day Saints appears similar to Christianity on the surface but is very different in theology underneath. It is considered to be a cult because it believes in a different Jesus than the Bible. For better understanding of the key differences between Christianity and the Latter Day Saints, read appendix A in my book *The Intercessors Handbook*.

8. "When you become baptized in the Holy Spirit, you will speak in a brand-new language; only it is a heavenly language, not a natural one." Eivaz, *Glory Carriers*, 19. For more instruction about receiving your prayer language, read the appendix of *Glory Carriers*, entitled "Receiving Your Spiritual Language through Holy Spirit Baptism."

9. Jennifer Eivaz, *Seeing the Supernatural* (Minneapolis: Chosen, 2017), 151. Also available at https://www.jennifereivaz.com/2019/12/02/can-a-christian-be-demon-possessed-2/.

10. "Derek Prince: War on Earth," YouTube video, 10:10, posted by Filip Peoski, September 8, 2008, https://www.youtube.com/watch?.

11. "Renounce meaning," Your Dictionary, https://www.yourdictionary.com/renounce.

12. "Astral projection (*n.*)," *The Merriam-Webster.com Dictionary*, https://www.merriam-webster.com/dictionary/astral%20projection.

13. "For God has not given us a spirit of fear, but of power and of love and of a sound mind" (2 Timothy 1:7).

14. "And behold, there was a woman who had a spirit of infirmity eighteen years, and was bent over and could in no way raise herself up" (Luke 13:11).

15. "'Not like the covenant which I made with their fathers on the day I took them by the hand to bring them out of the land of Egypt, My covenant which they broke, although I was a husband to them,' declares the LORD" (Jeremiah 31:32 NASB); "for your husband is your Maker" (Isaiah 54:5 NASB).

16. "You shall not bow down to them nor serve them. For I, the LORD your God, am a jealous God, visiting the iniquity of the fathers upon the children to the third and fourth generations of those who hate Me" (Deuteronomy 5:9).

17. Jeremiah 31:31–33 (NASB):

"Behold, days are coming," declares the LORD, "when I will make a new covenant with the house of Israel and with the house of Judah, not like the covenant which I made with their fathers in the day I took them by the hand to bring them out of the land of Egypt, My covenant which they broke, although I was a husband to them," declares the LORD. "For this is the covenant which I will make with the house of Israel after those days," declares the LORD: "I will put My law within them and write it on their heart; and I will be their God, and they shall be My people."

18. Jeffrey Kranz, "What's a Covenant? A Quick Definition and Overview," The Beginner's Guide to the Bible, October 20, 2013, https://overviewbible.com/covenant/.

19. Ibid.

20. "And this she did for many days. But Paul, greatly annoyed, turned and said to the spirit, 'I command you in the name of Jesus Christ to come out of her.' And he came out that very hour" (Acts 16:18).

Chapter 7 Healing the Jezebel-Afflicted Soul

1. "By faith Enoch was taken away so that he did not see death, 'and was not found, because God had taken him'; for before he was taken he had this testimony, that he pleased God" (Hebrews 11:5); "It came to pass, when the LORD was about to take up Elijah into heaven by a whirlwind, that Elijah went with Elisha from Gilgal. . . . Then it happened, as they continued on and talked, that suddenly a chariot of fire appeared with horses of fire, and separated the two of them; and Elijah went up by a whirlwind into heaven" (2 Kings 2:1, 11).

2. "Ahab told Jezebel all that Elijah had done, also how he had executed all the prophets with the sword. Then Jezebel sent a messenger to Elijah, saying, 'So let the gods do to me, and more also, if I do not make your life as the life of one of them by tomorrow about this time'" (1 Kings 19:1–2).

3. Anita Alexander, "The Returning of Fathers and Restoration of Families," The Elijah List, September 28, 2020, https://www.elijahlist.com /words/display_word.html?ID=24353; Max Fox and Nathan Altshuler, "Elijah: We Need You," March 24, 2018, https://www.jpost.com/opinion /elijah-we-need-you-546989; "The Messiah Would Be Preceded by Elijah the Prophet," Jews for Jesus, https://jewsforjesus.org/jewish-resources/mes sianic-prophecy/the-messiah-would-be-preceded-by-elijah-the-prophet/.

4. John Paul Jackson, *UnMasking the Jezebel Spirit* (Flower Mound, Tex.: Streams Ministries International, 2002), Kindle edition, 2.

5. "Jezebel Spirit in Men and Women," Curt Landry Ministries, February 27, 2020, https://www.curtlandry.com/jezebel-spirit-in-men/#.YGey 5i1h1pQ.

6. Melinda Smith, M.A. and Lawrence Robinson, "Narcissistic Personality Disorder," HelpGuide, July 2020, https://www.helpguide.org /articles/mental-disorders/narcissistic-personality-disorder.htm; "Narcissism: Symptoms and Signs," WebMD, December 2, 2020, https://www .webmd.com/mental-health/narcissism-symptoms-signs; Neal Chester, "The Narcissist's Origin: Exposing Jezebel, Part 1," Let's Please God, February, 12, 2020, https://www.letspleasegod.com/exposing-narcissist -part-1/; Diana Rasmussen, "Jezebels are Androgynous Narcissists," *Finding Hope in This Crazy World* (blog), https://dianarasmussen.com /jezebels-are-androgynous-narcissists/.

7. Jackson, *Unmasking the Jezebel Spirit*, 3.

8. Eivaz, *Seeing the Supernatural*, Kindle edition, 128.

9. "What Did Jesus Mean When He Said It Is Easier for a Camel to Go through the Eye of a Needle Than for a Rich Man to Get into Heaven?" Got Questions, https://www.gotquestions.org/camel-eye-needle.html.

10. Jackson, *UnMasking the Jezebel Spirit*, 2.

11. "Jezebel Spirit in Men and Women," Curt Landry Ministries.

Chapter 8 Freedom from Shame

8. "When there are spirits that go from generation to generation, manifesting on a piece of land, or in an actual family or bloodline, those spirits are called *familiar spirits*." Lance Wallnau, "Breaking Off Familiar Spirits," https://lancewallnau.com/breaking-off-familiar-spirits/.

2. Mary C. Lamia, Ph.D., "Shame: A Concealed, Contagious, and Dangerous Emotion," *Psychology Today*, April 4, 2011, https://www.psych ologytoday.com/us/blog/intense-emotions-and-strong-feelings/201104 /shame-concealed-contagious-and-dangerous-emotion.

3. Darlene Lancer, JD, MFT, "What Is Toxic Shame?" Psych Central, May 17, 2016, https://psychcentral.com/lib/what-is-toxic-shame#4.

4. I have heard this taught from different pulpits over the years but cannot remember who said it. Here are two links that support the suggestion: "Adam and Eve Clothed in Light before the Fall—Origin of This Belief?," Stack Exchange: Christianity, https://christianity.stack exchange.com/questions/47688/adam-and-eve-clothed-in-light-before -the-fall-the-origin-of-teaching; Ron Bateman, "Clothed in Glory," Revival Hut.com, September 10, 2017, http://revivalhut.com/clothed-in-glory/.

5. "5849. atar," *Strong's Concordance*, Bible Hub, http://biblehub.com /hebrew/5849.htm.

6. "5849. atar," *Strong's Exhaustive Concordance*, Bible Hub, http:// biblehub.com/hebrew/5849.htm.

7. To understand how trauma affects your physical body, read Bessel van der Kolk and Sean Pratt's *The Body Keeps the Score*, 1st ed. (New York: Viking; 2014).

Chapter 9 Defeating the Spirit of Fear

1. What happened to me was the result of the Holy Spirit's gift of discerning of spirits in operation. This gift is one of the nine gifts of the Spirit listed in 1 Corinthians 12:7–10 and is the supernatural ability to distinguish between spirits—divine, demonic or human. This gift is essential for those who are inner healing and deliverance ministers as it supernaturally reveals true heart conditions and various spirits needing to be addressed.

2. "The man's body shook violently in spasms, and the demon hurled him to the floor until it finally came out of him with a deafening shriek!" (Mark 1:26 TPT).

3. The Bible teaches us to forgive people who have harmed us because we will remain imprisoned and tormented if we hold on to offenses (see Matthew 18:21–25).

4. A prayer of repentance should be sincere and simple. For example, "Lord Jesus, I repent for watching horror movies. I have sinned against You and ask for Your forgiveness."

5. Joan Hunter, *Annihilate Fear* (Pinehurst, Tex.: Joan Hunter Ministries, 2021), Kindle edition, 23–24.

6. Ibid., 24.

7. Polly Tig, "What's the Difference Between Healthy Fear and Phobia," Anxiety, Panic, and Health, https://anxietypanichealth.com/2019 /07/26/whats-the-difference-between-healthy-fear-and-phobia.

8. Wikipedia contributors, "Scopophobia," *Wikipedia, The Free Encyclopedia*, https://en.wikipedia.org/wiki/Scopophobia.

9. "Y2K Bug," https://www.nationalgeographic.org/encyclopedia /Y2K-bug.

10. Lisa Miller, "Preacher Takes on Y2K Bug to Stop the Apocalyptic Panic," *Wall Street Journal*, January 21, 1999, https://www.wsj.com/articles /SB916814628926523000; Rob Boston, "Apocalypse Now?" Americans United for Separation of Church and State, March 1999, https://www .au.org/church-state/march-1999-church-state/featured/apocalypse-now.

11. National Paralegal College, "The Subprime Mortgage Crisis: Causes and Lessons Learned-Module 4 of 5," Law Shelf Educational Media, https://lawshelf.com/videocoursesmoduleview/the-subprime -mortgage-crisis-causes-and-lessons-learned-module-4-of-5/; Elinore Longobardi, "How 'Subprime' Crushed 'Predatory,'" *Columbia Journalism Review*, September/October 2009, https://archives.cjr.org/feature /how_subprime_crushed_predatory_1.php.

12. Jimmy Evans (@PsJimmyEvans), "Fear is a prophet spirit from hell. It tells us lies about the future to get us to react in fear & not obey by faith. Defeat fear by faith," Twitter, July 18, 2012, 7:47 a.m., https:// twitter.com/PsJimmyEvans/status/225557370154131457.

13. This is based on the parable of the sower: "The sower sows the word" (Mark 4:14).

14. "So then faith comes by hearing, and hearing by the word of God" (Romans 10:17).

15. "Now faith is the substance of things hoped for, the evidence of things not seen. For by it the elders obtained a good testimony" (Hebrews 11:1–2).

16. "To what shall we liken the kingdom of God? Or with what parable shall we picture it? It is like a mustard seed which, when it is sown on the ground, is smaller than all the seeds on earth; but when it is sown, it grows up and becomes greater than all herbs, and shoots out large branches, so that the birds of the air may nest under its shade" (Mark 4:30–32); "Because of your unbelief; for assuredly, I say to you, if you have faith as a mustard seed, you will say to this mountain, 'Move from here to there,' and it will move; and nothing will be impossible for you" (Matthew 17:20).

In Remembrance

1. Mental Health and Dissociative Amnesia," WebMD, April 21, 2019, https://www.webmd.com/mental-health/dissociative-amnesia#1:

Dissociative amnesia is not the same as simple amnesia, which involves a loss of information from memory, usually as the result of disease or injury to the brain. With dissociative amnesia, the memories still exist but are deeply buried within the person's mind and cannot be recalled. However, the memories might resurface on their own or after being triggered by something in the person's surroundings.

Jennifer Eivaz is a minister and international conference speaker with a heart to equip the Church in the supernatural and for raising up passionate and effective prayer. She is a regular contributor to Charisma Online and The Elijah List, has been featured on several Christian television shows, hosts the popular podcast *Take Ten With Jenn* and has authored several bestselling books. Jennifer lives with her husband, Ron, and their two children in Turlock, California, where she serves as co-pastor at Harvest Church.

To find out more about Jennifer and her ministry, you can visit her online:

Website: www.jennifereivaz.com
YouTube: Jennifer Eivaz
Facebook: www.facebook.com/jennifereivaz/
Twitter and Instagram: @PrayingProphet
TikTok: @jennifereivaz

Harvest Church
225 Fourth Street
Turlock, CA 95380
www.harvestturlock.org

More from Jennifer Eivaz

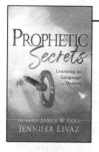
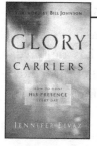